DEBBIE DEL...

D1062483

THE COMPONENTS
OF
SYNCHRONIZED
SWIMMING

THE COMPONENTS
OF
SYNCHRONIZED
SWIMMING

Frances Jones

> *Past National Chairman, AAU Competitive Synchronized Swimming*

Joyce Lindeman

> *Associate Professor of Physical Education*
> *University of Michigan*

PRENTICE-HALL, INC., *Englewood Cliffs, New Jersey*

Library of Congress Cataloging in Publication Data

JONES, FRANCES, date
    The components of synchronized swimming.

    Bibliography: p.
    1. Synchronized swimming. I. Lindeman, Joyce,
date   joint author. II. Title.
GV837.J63   797.2′1   74-16087
ISBN 0-13-164814-4

ⓒ 1975 by
PRENTICE-HALL, INC.
Englewood Cliffs, New Jersey

All rights reserved. No part of this book
may be reproduced in any way or by any means
without permission in writing from the publisher.

Printed in the United States of America.

10 9 8 7 6 5 4 3 2 1

PRENTICE-HALL INTERNATIONAL, INC., London
PRENTICE-HALL OF AUSTRALIA, PTY. LTD., Sydney
PRENTICE-HALL OF CANADA, LTD., Toronto
PRENTICE-HALL OF INDIA PRIVATE LIMITED, New Delhi
PRENTICE-HALL OF JAPAN, INC., Tokyo

To all the synchronized swimmers,
teachers and coaches in the high school, university,
and athletic club levels,
who have throughout the years
stimulated our interest in synchronized swimming

CONTENTS

6

DEVELOPMENTAL MOVEMENTS FOR SYNCHRONIZED SWIMMERS 148

7

COACHING THE COMPETITIVE SYNCHRONIZED SWIMMER 176

8

THE ROUTINE CHOREOGRAPHY 195

9

JUDGING COMPETITIVE SYNCHRONIZED SWIMMING 199

PREFACE

The Components of Synchronized Swimming, which was written for high school and university teachers of physical education and for coaches of competitive synchronized swimming, covers both aspects of synchronized swimming: the water show production and the treatment of the activity for competition. The concept of this text involves a classroom progression in which the "part-to-whole" method is recommended for the beginner and is described in such a way that it serves as a new scientific approach to the teaching of synchronized swimming. The total scope of this book represents a broad composite of components collected during twenty years of teaching in high schools and universities, as well as of coaching nationally rated competitive swimmers. The research findings contained in this text are applicable to the present-day training methods used in competitive synchronized swimming.

We wish to express our sincere appreciation to the many individuals who made this book possible: to Professor Diane Ross, Physical Education Department of the California State University, Fullerton, for her valuable expertise in counsel in the field of kinesiology; to Professor Beverly Jones, English Department of Oakland University, Rochester, Michigan, who so generously contributed her time in editing and proofreading the manuscript; and to Mrs. Marie Lacey, secretary at the University of Michigan, who typed the manuscript.

A special gratitude is extended to Miss Gail Johnson, National AAU synchronized swimming champion and member of the Santa Clara Aquamaids; to

Miss Kay McDonald of the Garden City Parks and Recreation; and to Miss Leyla Aldikacti of the Michigan Aquarius Club, who executed the stable positions and figure transitions for our photographers.

We wish to thank our film specialists, Mr. Allen Noftz, Miss Helen Deckert, and Mr. Bruce Moxley; also our sincere thanks to Miss Kathy Ryan, University of Michigan, for the illustrations of the numerous movements from which the figure drawings were adapted.

We also wish to express our gratitude to: Mr. Will Luick of Jole Company, San Jose, California, for loop films and guidance in photographic procedures; Mrs. Judith Sarver, formerly with the Dance Department, University of Windsor, Canada; Miss Cynthia Kincaid and Miss Margaret Pittenger, Registered Physical Therapists, who gave us guidance with developmental movements; and the Aquarius and Michifish synchronized swimming clubs coached by the authors. The efforts of all other persons who collected data in preparation for this teaching manual are greatly appreciated.

Frances Jones
Joyce Lindeman

THE COMPONENTS OF SYNCHRONIZED SWIMMING

1

SYNCHRONIZED SWIMMING: ORGANIZATIONAL STRUCTURE

As an activity, synchronized swimming may be considered a highly competitive individual or team sport or a highly skilled art form. In every sense of the word the quality of movement, the flow of patterns, the portrayal of a mood, idea, image or impression make synchronized swimming aesthetically appealing. At its highest level it demands quality swimming, breath control, acute timing, coordination, and strength, all of which identify the activity as a competitive sport.

Although the high-level performance represents a sophisticated training program on a daily basis, the authors nevertheless feel that the benefits of the activity should not be restricted to the nation's most accomplished swimmers. The physical requirements of the sport are so varied as to be adaptable to swimmers of all ages and skill levels, so as to permit some degree of pleasurable achievement for all participants. Of further benefit to all swimmers is the opportunity to exercise their creative powers in the composition of patterns and rhythmic responses that contribute to the artistic nature of the performance. Thus synchronized swimming can be enjoyed both by the participant and the general public through the medium of the water show production, perhaps a culminating event of a season's training that provides motivation for quality instruction and swimmer achievement. Because of its potential enhancement of the physical and emotional well-being of all participants, synchronized swimming should be incorporated into all aquatic programs: recreational and educational as well as competitive.

HISTORY

Historically, synchronized swimming is a relatively new aquatic activity, which is thought to have had its roots in Europe. One of its first forms was floating in formation to a musical background. Katharine Curtis was the originator of synchronized swimming in the United States; she organized the first known swimming club for women at the University of Chicago in 1923.[1] This group executed tricks and float formations, and its activity was first called water ballet. In the beginning, music was used only for a background; later, swimmers began to plan their movements to coincide with the rhythm of the music. In 1934, Katharine Curtis's group, the Modern Mermaids, performed at the Century of Progress Exhibition in the Chicago World's Fair. Thereafter, enthusiasm grew quickly.[2] The name *synchronized swimming* was first coined by Norman Ross and used in publicity at the fair.[3] In 1939, the first dual meet was held, and in 1941, the Amateur Athletic Union accepted synchronized swimming as a competitive sport and drew up rules to govern its competition. National championships have been held since 1945. In 1951, synchronized swimming was demonstrated at the Pan-American Games and by 1955, was an official sport of the Games. Several countries have been interested in the acceptance of synchronized swimming as an Olympic sport. Synchronized swimmers have exhibited at the 1952, 1956, 1960, 1964, 1968, and 1972 Olympic Games. Rules governing the sport have been drawn up and accepted by the Federation Internationale de Natation Amateur, the international governing body. Synchronized swimming enthusiasts are hopeful of someday finding synchronized swimming among the listed sports in the Olympic Games. Growth and popularity in the sport can be seen throughout the world as evidenced by the 1971 FINA report, which revealed that twenty-six nations have synchronized swimming programs, and eighteen nations are conducting annual championships.[4]

The International Academy of Aquatic Art is another organization promoting synchronized swimming. Founded by Beulah Gundling in 1955, the academy emphasizes synchronized swimming as an art form rather than a

[1] Hollis Tait, John Shaw, and Katherine Ley, *A Manual of Physical Education Activities,* 3rd ed. (Philadelphia and London: W. B. Saunders Co., 1967).

[2] Katharine Curtis, *A Source Book of Water Pageantry* (Chicago: The College Press, 1936).

[3] Juliane Von Wietersheim, "An Approach to the Teaching of Composition in a Synchronized Swimming Course." Master's thesis, Smith College, 1955.

[4] Dawn Bean, *Synchro-Info,* Vol. IX, no. 6, December, 1971.

competitive sport. The IAAA conducts annual festivals giving participants an opportunity to present their compositions for evaluation and awards.[5]

ORGANIZATIONS THAT SPONSOR
SYNCHRONIZED SWIMMING COMPETITIONS

Amateur Athletic Union

The Amateur Athletic Union is the governing body for amateur synchronized swimming contests in the United States. Such contests are held annually in various parts of the country. A bona fide competitor, one who is an AAU registered athlete may enter these contests, providing certain qualifications are present. For example, except for age group and junior olympic competitions, a swimmer must be twelve years of age. The twelve-year-old qualifies for district competition in the district novice, junior, and senior divisions. A twelve-year-old may enter both junior and senior national meets when a qualifying score has been achieved at either a zone or regional meet.

The AAU national synchronized swimming committee has rules that govern the competitive events. Three classes of competition are recognized: the solo, duet, and team. When entered in any one of these classes, a swimming routine performed to music must be executed for a panel of trained judges. The swim routine must be so constructed that five schooled figures are incorporated in the choreography. The swim routine is judged in two parts: execution of figures, strokes and parts of each, and content (including various other elements such as variety, difficulty, and creativeness). Each swimmer is also expected to compete in the schooled figure event. Such figures may consist of required figures previously designated in the rules, or half optional and half required.

The final tally of points includes the scores received in the swimming routine and for the schooled figure event. The Official Synchronized Swimming Handbook, published by the AAU, furnishes complete rules and information regarding the conduct of these meets and each event therein.

Federation Internationale de Natation Amateur

The Federation Internationale de Natation (FINA) is the governing body for international competition in swimming and diving, water polo, and synchronized swimming. FINA rules are followed for the Pan American Games and all international meets. Furthermore, all of the countries affiliated with FINA conduct competitions according to FINA rules, whereas competitions in the United States follow AAU rules exclusively. The basic difference between AAU and FINA

---

[5] Beulah Gundling, *Exploring Aquatic Art* (Cedar Rapids, Iowa: International Acadamy of Aquatic Art, 1963).

competition is found in the descriptions of figures and in the performance of a free routine devoid of the five required figures. Routines and figures are performed for a panel of judges. Routines are judged as a unit considering: the perfection of strokes, figures, and parts thereof; variety, difficulty, and pool patterns of the routine; synchronization of the swimmers, one with the others and also with the accompaniment; interpretation of the music; and manner of presentation. Figures are judged only on execution. The FINA committee selects the judges based on a list submitted from the countries entered.[6]

International Academy of Aquatic Art

The International Academy of Aquatic Art (IAAA) is an organization that conducts festivals and symposiums annually and draws participants nationally and internationally. The IAAA emphasizes execution, creativity, and expression in the water, with less emphasis on competition between swimmers. Compositions are classified as solo, duet, trio, and group, and may be performed by males or females. Performers present a free composition to a panel of seven critics to evaluate according to its artistic merits. Compositions receive one of four possible ratings (IAAA, AAA, AA, and A), and swimmers meet with the critics after their performances to discuss and evaluate the compositions.[7]

Division of Girls' and Women's Sports

The Division of Girls' and Women's Sport (DGWS) is an educational organization designed to serve the needs and interests of professional leaders in schools, colleges, recreational associations, and other clubs and agencies. The DGWS synchronized swimming guidelines are based on the official AAU synchronized swimming rules. When conducting school meets, DGWS suggests following their established source book, *Guidelines for Interscholastic Athletic Programs,* published in three booklets: for junior high girls, high school girls, and women. Events can then be sanctioned by DGWS rather than AAU, insuring closer attention to school eligibility rules and saving the AAU fee for sanctioning events. A further power recently gained by the DGWS is the right to rate judges for their own competitions.

Midwest Intercollegiate Synchronized Swimming Competition

The midwest colleges hold an annual meet in the spring. This competition follows the AAU rules modified to meet college needs. These modifications have been adapted from the FINA and IAAA rules, and the meets are sanctioned

---

[6] *Federation Internationale de Natation Amateur.* Handbook, printed in Japan, 1969–72.

[7] Gundling, *Exploring Aquatic Art.*

by the DGWS. Competition consists of solo, duet, trio, and team events performed by male and female swimmers. Routines are free routines, and the figure competition is optional. The figure competition is divided into novice, junior, and senior events, and no more than three swimmers from any college may enter each division. Each college may enter five routines with no more than two in any one division. AAU, DGWS, or IAAA judges are selected for the meets, and judging is based on three categories: content, synchronization, and execution. Figure scores are not added to the routine scores in these competitions.

OTHER GROUPS THAT PROMOTE SYNCHRONIZED SWIMMING

Several states are promoting synchonized swimming by various agencies other than the AAU. As an example, Michigan has formed the Michigan Synchronized Swimming Coaches' Association for the purpose of conducting clinics (figures, routine, water show, judging, etc.) and sponsoring competitions (novice, high school, college, and AAU). This group is composed of high school, college, private club, recreational, and AAU synchronized swimming coaches. The coaches' association prints a newsletter and periodically brings in resource people and top swimmers to stimulate interest and improve quality. All coaches are encouraged to participate in planning and teaching at clinics. Many coaches and students have become qualified judges through the judges' training and testing clinics sponsored by this organization. Both DGWS and AAU ratings are offered, making it possible to have qualified judges at all meets.

In addition to state and/or association clubs, some city parks and recreation departments are promoting this sport through summer programs. One in particular is the Omaha (Nebraska) Recreation Department. Pools within designated locations compete against each other on certain days. Each team is independent and the swimmer represents the individual pool. Each pool checks basic skills, teaches required figures, introduces optional figures, and prepares routines. The skill sheets are devised according to AAU figure categories, and pool coaches evaluate individuals on the team and grade figures accordingly on a scale of zero to ten in preparation for the routines against other pools. Skill sheets include four levels: novice-beginner, junior-intermediate, senior-advanced, and master-superior. After careful examination by the coach, a certificate is awarded. A grade of five must be earned on a certain percentage of the figures before promotion to the next skill sheet. Each competitor is evaluated daily in the individual pools; therefore, figure competition is waived for routine competition. The first round of competition for the summer program consists of solos and duets; the second round is for duets, trios, and teams. At the end of the summer, city-wide championships are conducted, and include solos, duets, trios, and teams. The response and enthusiasm for this program has been exceptional.[8]

[8] Dawn Bean, *Synchro-Info,* Vol. ix, no. 6, December, 1971.

SUGGESTED GUIDELINES FOR COMPETITION

All synchronized swimming coaches should have *The Amateur Athletic Union Official Synchonized Swimming Handbook* and follow the text as a base for all competition. High schools and colleges should follow the DGWS guidelines for interscholastic competition. These two sources should govern competitive meets. Additional modification in these rules should follow AAU or FINA requirements.

SCHOOLED FIGURE COMPETITION

The name *schooled figure* refers to sequences of movement that follow a prescribed pattern. The figure is performed in the water in a manner specified by the organization or governing body of the sport or art form. The schooled figures are given such picturesque names as Dolphin, Catalina, Gaviata, Flamingo, Porpoise, and Albatross. However, these names do not in any manner explain the execution of these figures.

The AAU divides the figures into four categories: ballet leg group, dolphin group, somersault group, and diverse group. As in competitive diving, each figure has an assigned number and degree of difficulty; in this case, from 1.1 to 2.2.

The figure competition requires a competitor to perform compulsory schooled figures, selected from an established list, and/or a certain number of optional figures; the number of each is found in the current rule book. For example, AAU Senior National Competition requires six compulsory schooled figures drawn prior to the meet, whereas other AAU competitions require the execution of three specific figures listed as compulsory and either two or three optionals, each of which must be from a different figure grouping.

The figures are performed before a panel of judges and awarded points for execution (zero to ten). The design and control of the figure are considered of equal importance in arriving at the judges' awards. Design includes horizontal or vertical, pike, tuck, or arched body positions. Control includes body extensions, smooth transitions, elevation of the body above the surface, compactness of positions, and effortless execution. Competitive schooled figures are to be performed from a stationary position (without a stroke or traveling) by a swimmer in a one-piece, dark-colored suit devoid of club emblems. Only in AAU and FINA competition is the figure competition considered an integral part of the meet so that the figure scores are totaled with the routine scores.

ROUTINES AND ROUTINE COMPETITION

A routine or composition consists of creative figures, standard and hybrid strokes, and propulsive techniques aesthetically combined and synchronized to a musical accompaniment. Routines are classified solo, duet, trio, and team (group) events. A team consists of at least four swimmers and generally not more than eight. (IAAA and Midwest Intercollegiates do not limit the number on a team.)

An AAU routine must include five required schooled figures to be listed and performed as described in the rules. All members of the routine must perform the five figures simultaneously, and these figures cannot include more than two from each figure group.

Only AAU and FINA routines have a specified time limit: four minutes for solos and duets and five minutes for team events, with a limit of twenty seconds for deck work. The timing of the routine begins and ends with the music. Penalties are given for overtime on the deck and/or in the water. IAAA and Midwest Intercollegiate competitions are free of time limitations and penalties.

An appropriate costume, depicting the general theme of the routine is worn. AAU routine competition is judged by a panel of five or seven judges. National competition requires seven judges. Judging is based on two categories: content and execution. Content includes synchronization, difficulty, variety, creative action, and fluidity of the routine; execution includes the performance of the schooled and/or hybrid figures, strokes, and propulsion techniques of the routine.

JUDGING SCHOOLED FIGURES AND ROUTINES

Schooled Figures

The judging of schooled figures follows the AAU judging rules, with very few exceptions. The figures are judged on a half point gradation scale, from zero to ten. As previously stated, the two essential components of an excellent figure consist of design (five points) and control (five points). The following is the scale used to judge figures: [9]

Excellent
Design—near perfection of body position   9–10
Control—effortless, near perfection

Good
Design—good body positions   7–8½
Control—above satisfactory

Satisfactory
Design—average   5–6½
Control—average

[9] *Official Amateur Athletic Union of the United States Synchronized Swimming Handbook* (Indianapolis, Ind.: AAU, 1972).

Unsatisfactory
    Design—unsteady body position   3–4½
    Control—weak

Deficient
    Design—figure recognizable, major deficiencies   ½–2½
    Control—very poor

Failed
    Unrecognizable as a listed figure or performed other than listed   0
    Minor infractions not to be judged zero

Routines

    IAAA, FINA, Midwest Intercollegiate, and AAU routines are judged differently because of their diverse categories. In essence, the judges are looking for approximately the same elements; therefore, only a brief explanation of the AAU routine judging will be presented.
    The difficulty of judging routines is primarily that it is by nature subjective; the judge should not be affected by the music, costume, or the appearance of the performance. The judges flash two scores at the completion of the routine, one for the content and one for the execution. Scoring is from zero to ten and in one-tenth–point gradations. When judging content, the breakdown is as follows: [10]

Content Scoring	*Solo*	*Duet*	*Team*
1. Synchronization (one with the other and with the accompaniment)	1		4
2. Construction			
a. Creative action	2		1
b. Fluidity	2		1
c. Difficulty	4		3
d. Variety	1		1

    Judging of execution includes all elements in the total routine: schooled and/or hybrid figures, swimming strokes, and propulsion techniques. These are graded from a standpoint of perfection. The execution score is from zero to ten in 1/10 points gradation and is broken down as follows: [11]

[10] Ibid.
[11] Ibid.

EXECUTION SCORING

Excellent	9	— 10
Good	7	— 8.9
Satisfactory	5	— 6.9
Unsatisfactory	3	— 4.9
Deficient	.5 —	2.9
Failed	0	

SYNCHRONIZED SWIMMING JUDGES' RATINGS

Amateur Athletic Union Rating

NATIONAL JUDGE

To become a national AAU judge one must first be recommended to the National Testing Committee as a senior association judge and have attended Senior National Championships during the past three years. The testing includes passing with ninety percent or higher, figure identification, and a written examination. Next, a candidate must practice judge (and pass) the following activities at two Senior National Championships within a two-year period:

  a. Twenty solos, twenty duets, and twenty teams in the preliminaries (if one area is failed, the candidate may judge that area in the finals)
  b. Twelve of each figure (there are six figures), for a total of thirty-six

And, finally, one must pass an oral examination administered by a panel of AAU nationally rated judges.

This rating is valid for two years, qualifying the official to be elected by the coaches to judge at any AAU meet while in attendance. To retain this rating the judge must pass the written and figure-recognition test every two years, attend Senior National Championships at least twice during three years, and receive good or excellent rating in judging from the Judges' Evaluation Committee. After a judge passes the written test three times, she needs only to be present at one senior national meet per year (she does not need to judge). If a rating expires, two Senior National Championships cannot pass by before renewing, or a judge will need to begin again.

LOCAL ASSOCIATION JUDGE

The Local AAU Judges' rating permits judging at all levels except the national level. A written examination and figure-identification test must be passed with a score of ninety percent or higher. Furthermore, a candidate must pass a test in the practice judging of routines, compulsory figures, and optional figures. Usually a National Judge within each association will conduct judges' training clinics and set up testing dates. This rating is valid for two years, and renewal is by completing the same sequence. Steps are presently being taken toward uniformity in judging standards and testing on the local levels.

REFEREES

The National AAU Rating Committee is devising a testing program for referees.

Division of Girls' and Women's Sports Judging Rating

The DGWS Synchronized Swimming Judges' rating is valid for two years and is administered by local county boards of DGWS Officials. This rating allows the official to judge at all association AAU meets, Midwest Intercollegiate, high school, and college meets but does not, usually, allow a person to judge at IAAA or AAU senior or junior national meets.

To obtain this rating, a candidate must pass a uniform test: figure identification viewed on an opaque projector, and routine judging of solo, duet, and teams as viewed on film. There are five levels of judges, depending on scoring and age: [12]

National official—at least twenty years old—may judge anywhere in the United States.

        Theory examination—minimum score of 82
        Practical examination—minimum score of 85
        Average score   85

Junior national official—under twenty years old.

        Same as national official

Local official—no age requirement—may judge in interschool or recreation meets.

        Theory examination—minimum score of 78
        Practical examination—minimum score of 80
        Average score   80

Associate official—no age requirement.

        Theory examination—minimum score of 74
        Practical examination—minimum score of 75
        Average score   75

Intramural official—no age requirement.

        Theory examination—minimum score of 70
        Practical examination—minimum score of 70
        Average score   70

[12] American Association for Health, Physical Education and Recreation, *Aquatics Guide* (Washington, D.C.: AAHPER), July, 1969–71.

After five consecutive renewals, the judge is given a rating of honorary National Judge.

The National DGWS Synchronized Swimming Committee is in the process of devising testing procedures for referees.

International Academy of Aquatic Art Critic Rating

The *critic* is the official who rates an IAAA composition. According to the IAAA bylaws, an aquatic art critic is: "A flexible-minded person of mature judgment who has been approved by the Board of Control of the IAAA." Also according to the IAAA bylaws, the method used by the critic to evaluate the synchronized swimming routine shall be as follows:

> The critic shall give a single rating covering his evaluation of the composition. The composition shall be considered by the critic in its entirety. His single award shall cover all aspects of the composition without attempting to assign specific weights to any one of them. He shall analyze the *performance,* not its components, in the light of his personal experience.

Such ratings are given only at International Festivals and are optional.

2

SYNCHRONIZED SWIMMING: DEVELOPING FUNDAMENTAL SKILLS

In this context, *fundamental* refers to a general grouping of skills basic to the sport. The term *skill* refers to specific movement sequences and patterns used by the synchronized swimmer. Each fundamental skill is performed under comparatively minimal resistance (less difficult) as compared to the advanced skills of increased resistance (greater difficulty). Examples of these skills are breathing and breath holding, floating in the front and back layout positions, propulsion sculling, scoop and pull, modified standard swimming strokes, egg beater, and simple schooled figures. Although several of these skills are used in other sports and have been analyzed in other texts, when applied to synchronized swimming, specific identifying characteristics are worth noting. The following information focuses on improvement of each fundamental skill.

BREATHING AND BREATH HOLDING

Because nose clips are worn during both the figures and routine performance, synchronized swimmers inhale and exhale through the mouth. Unlike the rhythmic breathing used by speed swimmers, the synchronized swimmer is called upon to hold the breath numerous times for ten to fifteen seconds and, less frequently, for periods of twenty to thirty seconds. Care must be given to teach the synchronized swimmer to perform a schooled figure with a normal-size breath before executing lengthy transitions under water. An overload of air greatly increases buoyancy and very often forces stiffness through the shoulder girdle. In addition, the water pressure adds to the discomfort of holding an over-size breath. It is therefore necessary to develop the endurance for holding an adequate breath while performing underwater figures. Endurance may be developed through numerous aquatic activities as listed.

1. Condition the swimmer to breath holding while sitting on the pool floor in shallow water. Begin with ten-second breath holding. Repeat after a fifteen-second rest. The teacher may count the seconds for the swimmer while using an underwater speaker.

2. Progress by requiring the swimmer to cross the width of the pool under water. Allow the swimmer to return at the surface still holding the breath. This activity is an over-and-under exercise adaptable to large classes. When the class is twenty or more in number, half the group may pass over on the surface while the other half is returning under water.

3. Make a game out of breath holding. Pom-Pom Swim Away under water is fun. One swimmer is "it." The other swimmers must change goals and not be caught.

4. Breath-holding endurance is increased gradually by swimming longer distances under water. The important element to stress is relaxation while holding a normal-size breath. Because some swimmers black out during underwater drills, careful guarding of the pool is advised.

FLOATING IN THE LAYOUT POSITION

The ability to float enables the synchronized swimmer to perform the back and front layout positions (arms over head or at the side). To float, the swimmer is dependent upon air in the lungs, stability of body alignment, and the specific gravity of the body mass.[1] A brief analysis of the front and back layout floating positions may be explained to the class as follows. The abdominal muscles must be shortened and counterbalanced by the hip extensors. The result of this action will be the stabilizing of the pelvic area (center of gravity) while holding it near the water surface. During the back layout the head is pressed into the water by contracting the muscles adjoining the base of the skull. The chin will be level and the ears under water. The swimmer will feel stretched from both ends of the body. In the front layout, the breath is held while the face is in the water, ears in line with the shoulders, and abdominals shortened to elevate the level body line. The teacher may include other helpful suggestions to assist the floating body; i.e., during the back layout (arms above head), raise hands above the water to

[1] George Rackham, *Synchronized Swimming* (London: Faber & Faber Ltd., 1968).

assist in keeping the feet at the surface. Hold the hips at the surface by sucking the diaphragm into the rib cage; press the hips upward until the top of the thighs are airborne. Hold the feet up by tightening the hip flexors. The lateral muscles of the trunk must be equal in tension to prevent the body from rolling side to side. Approximately one-fiftieth of the body should be at the surface while maintaining the horizontal floating positions.[2]

PROPULSION SCULLING

Unique to the sport of synchronized swimming, propulsion sculling is an inward and outward rotary action of the forearm and hand accompanied by flexion and extension at the elbow joint. The hand is an extension of the forearm and slightly adducts and abducts during the propulsion pattern. Propulsion sculling is used at the hips and beyond the head when in a prone or supine layout position. The body will travel in the opposite direction to the direction of pressure exerted by the palms of the hands. This movement enables the swimmer (while holding the torso horizontal) to travel headfirst or feet-first, to slip sideways in the water and/or turn around the dorso-ventral axis. When the body is positioned vertically in the water with the head toward the pool floor, propulsion sculling is used to turn the swimmer around the longitudinal axis of the body.

MOVEMENT ABOUT THE BODY AXES

FIG. 1   Dorso-ventral

FIG. 2   Longitudinal

When teaching propulsion sculling, it is most important that the teacher is certain the swimmer understands the proper action for each lever involved: (part of the arm) hand, forearm, and upper arm. A descriptive movement analysis of the action of these levers is included in chapter 4. Propulsion sculling may be described as a small rapid pattern devoid of a recovery stage. When the arms are at the hips or over the head, pressure is exerted on the thumb edge of the hands as the forearms move outward from the body. Pressure is exerted

[2] Ibid.

on the little finger edge as the forearms flex. The upper arms remain stationary and do not give way to the pressure created at the hands. As these levers traverse the pattern, they move only slightly outside the elbows. When the body is horizontal (prone or supine), for teaching purposes, encourage the swimmer to exert greatest pressure on the edge of the hands adjacent to the body as the forearms are extending. This tip inhibits the use of a recovery phase that is often used by students until they have learned the complete mechanics of sculling. Under teacher guidance, following an explanation and demonstration of the sculling movement, direct the swimmer to practice the skill slowly. The teacher should approve the sculling action before the student attempts to increase the speed of the pattern. The elongated horizontal figure-eight pattern is approximately ten to twelve inches in total length. The fingers change depth approximately three inches as the forearm rotates about the elbow. As the sculling patterns are repeated with increased speed, the body will move more rapidly in its intended direction (as the speed of the pattern is doubled, the resistance created at the hand will increase fourfold). To propel a horizontal body position, the palms of the hands are nearly perpendicular to the line of travel. Although the wrists are held either flexed or hyperextended, they also perform subtle al-

FIG. 3   Hyperextended hand   FIG. 4   Flexed hand

ternating movements of adduction and abduction. Once the motor pattern appears to be developed, build strength and endurance by conducting speed sculling races. An event of this nature should be a part of each class period. Begin by racing across the width of the pool. A pool approximately forty feet wide should be traversed in eighteen seconds. Gradually increase the length of the course until seventy-five feet are sculled in approximately thirty seconds. The proportion of distance traveled over time reveals proficiency in propulsion sculling. As sculling times improve, introduce repeated lengths with less time to rest between races. This method of endurance training (known as interval training) is used in many sports to keep athletes in top condition.

The synchronized swimmer is rewarded and motivated when the speed sculling records are displayed in the pool area much the same as the records made by speed swimmers. Records may be posted frequently at the conclusion of a significant block of time. Post the name of the swimmer, the type of sculling (at the hips or over head), the distance, and the time.

To develop sculling strength, add weight by means of an airborne ballet leg or double ballet legs. Some success has been found in wearing ankle bands.

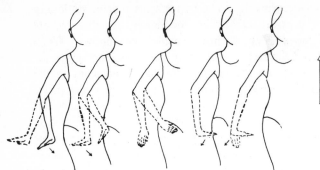

FIG. 5   Standard scull, back layout

FIG. 6   Reverse standard scull, back layout

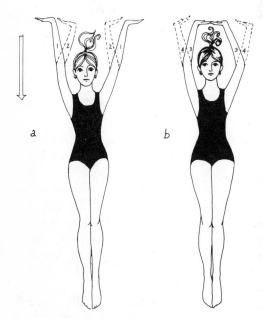

FIG. 7   Propeller scull, back layout

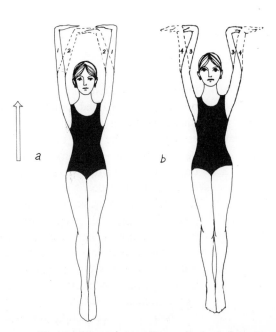

FIG. 8   Reverse propeller scull, back layout

Fig. 9   Standard scull, front layout

Fig. 11   Twist scull, vertical

Fig. 10   Propeller scull, front layout

A very practical method is to wear tennis shoes. When swimmers are able to carry double ballet legs the length of the pool (approximately seventy-five feet), keeping the water line near mid thigh, the swimmer has adequate strength for any propulsion sculling necessary in routine execution. *Power equals weight times distance over time.*

Obstacle races also develop sculling power. These activities stimulate enthusiasm while contributing to increased strength. Tug-of-war sculling in a chain is fun and adaptable to a competitive experience. Teams of four or five swimmers are connected in a back layout position. At the foot of each chain, swimmers connect ankle-to-ankle. Each chain has a goal toward which it will scull. The teacher gives the command to begin and allows thirty seconds for the contest or until one chain enters the goal area.

The authors suggest "speed pattern" sculling at the trough with the feet or the head maintaining contact with the pool wall. The swimmer must count the number of outward presses performed in a set time period. When in the back layout position, the approximate speed guide to work toward is eight complete figure-eight patterns every five seconds continued at this speed for thirty seconds. Because the speed of the sculling is relevant to support of weight, the swimmer must be proficient at speed sculling in the back layout, the position to which weight is added during the performance of schooled figures. When in the front layout, the speed of the pattern is decreased to approximately four patterns every five seconds, enough to support the floating body when stationary or traveling. Swimmers must learn to gauge the speed of sculling with the amount of resistance and/or weight to support. For example: when floating in the back layout, slow sculling is adequate. However, a more rapid pattern must be used to support a single ballet leg, whereas maximum speed and strength must accompany double ballet legs. To assist in pacing the swimmer, the teacher may count aloud each five seconds of sculling. The use of an underwater speaker or a percussive instrument will aid in timing this activity for the class.

THE SCOOP

The scoop is a propulsion arm pattern (see figures 12 and 13). It may follow a direct course of resistance or a weaving line (feathering). A large scoop involves the total arm from shoulder to finger tip. A small scoop of less range involves only movement of the forearm from elbow to finger tips. A scoop from either the shoulder or elbow exerts pressure against the water in a head-first direction. The scoop is used in several portions of figures during transitional movement; i.e., during the underwater passage of the body in the foot-first dolphin, the airborne arc of the leg in the swordfish and hightower, the tip up in the subcrane; when coupled with short pulls, the scoop also enhances the transition from front layout to front pike vertical (porpoise beginning).

OTHER PROPULSION PATTERNS

FIG. 12   Scoop, back layout

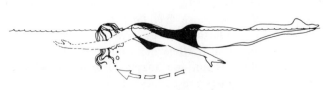

FIG. 13   Scoop, front layout

THE PULL

The pull, a propulsive arm pattern, is an important skill in a swimmer's repertoire of movement (see figures 14 and 15). Its direction of pressure is toward the feet although it may feather while on course. It may involve the total arm or only the forearm, as described. Swimmers most frequently use the total-arm pull when performing the audience-pleasing dolphin chain or pinwheel. Both the scoop and pull create intermittent drive. Each has a recovery stage. The teacher should caution the swimmer to make the recovery in the line of least resistance: to carefully draw the parts of the upper arm along the rib cage and then follow with a reach or stretch of the forearm. A proper recovery should not adversely affect the momentum of the body.

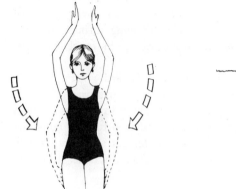

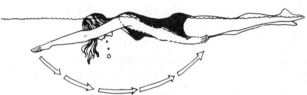

FIG. 15   Pull, front layout

FIG. 14   Pull, back layout

MODIFIED STANDARD SWIMMING STROKES

A prerequisite for synchronized swimming is the ability to execute the standard swimming strokes proficiently. Since these techniques are readily available in other texts, we shall discuss only the modifications, the hybridization, and the variations of standard strokes used in this particular sport.

The standard strokes are modified and adapted to the specific needs of the synchronized swimmer and are performed to music. The front crawl requires that the head be carried above the water with the chin at the surface or above. The hips may be somewhat deeper in the water, depending on the swimmer's ability to stretch the body and the power delivered in the kicking action.

When using any of the various rhythms, the tempo (speed) of the count must be agreed upon by the coach and the swimmer before the standard strokes are set to time. In a moderate-tempo four-four rhythm, the complete arm pattern of the front crawl may require four counts. One downbeat may be given for the lift of the elbow, a second beat for the forearm and hand to extend and enter the water (recovery phase), and two counts for the pull. This describes a full moderate four-four–time stroke. When this stroke is executed in "half time" (elbow lift on "and," the forearm extended on "one," the pull through the water executed on "and two"), the stroke movements become twice as fast. An attempt to execute this stroke in a quarter time would be disasterous.

Feathering during the front crawl (weaving the hand and forearm inward and outward on the down pull) is a common technique used when the tempo of the four-four rhythm is comparatively slow. Overuse of this technique becomes boring to watch unless the body is rapidly propelled by the legs. Too little movement in an aquatic environment tends to mesmerize the audience or the judge.

The crawl stroke is modified in its airborne pattern (recovery) by a straight arm lift from the shoulder accompanied by a high arc of the arm before the hand reenters the water. Such a stroke appears crisp and rapid when executed at a half-time tempo.

The back stroke is similar to the straight-arm crawl. The recovery phase of the stroke is exaggerated by a high arc of the arm traveling through the air, with an emphasis on the lift and a decrease in speed prior to its touchdown entrance into the water behind the head.

The crawl and back strokes become laborious and awkward when attempted at a quarter-time tempo (one count for each complete stroke pattern).

The breast stroke and side stroke are readily adaptable to various musical rhythms and are considered in good form when executed in a full- or half-time tempo. A rapid, moderate, or slow tempo of any rhythmical structure usually accommodates these strokes. Be sure the swimmer develops the side stroke on both the left and right sides.

Hybrids and Variations

The hybridization and variation of modified standard strokes are considered among the fundamental skills. When only parts of standard strokes are combined to form a new stroke pattern, the combination is a hybrid stroke, whereas when a modified stroke is performed using variations of movement during the recovery phase, the result is referred to as a variation stroke. Often parts of variation strokes are executed using a quarter-time or double-time tempo. Small movements of the hands or forearms are possible using either one count or a half count in a four-four rhythm of moderate tempo. Variation stroking provides a limitless opportunity for creative expression. Such creativity becomes an important element in the choreography of the routine and is a judging factor in routine competition.

EGG BEATER

Within the swimming routine, moments appear when the swimmer wishes to give propulsion or support to airborne arm and hand movements. These sequences usually occur when the body is vertical or near vertical with the head and shoulders above the water. The leg action must provide the necessary force to maintain the airborne weight devoid of bobbing. An alternating whip kick of the legs best describes the egg beater (a supportive leg pattern). While one leg applies pressure toward the pool floor, the other leg is making a recovery. The inside of the lower leg and foot serve as the area against which pressure is exerted. Pressure is toward the pool floor as the leg moves outward and down, followed by pressure on the outside edge of the foot as the action continues inward toward the mid-body line. The recovery is made from ankle to knee by sharply flexing the knee, moving the heel behind and outside the knee. During this circular motion, the upper leg is limited to inward and outward rotation at the hip socket. The following suggestions are given to aid the teaching of the egg-beater kick.

1. Direct the students to sit on the edge of the pool or bench facing the wall clock. Have them begin with the right leg. The starting position is a flexed hip and knee with the right heel pointing outward. This position is twelve o'clock on the dial. As the foot is pressed outward and downward the movement traces the face of the clock in a clockwise direction. When using the left leg the beginning position is assumed but the movement is counterclockwise.

2. While executing a reverse bicycle in the water, have swimmers hold the pool trough. Slowly move the heels farther and farther away from the mid-body line until the feet travel outside the width of the shoulders.

3. Move the class to deep water where swimmers may practice the entire sequence under the added stress of weight (raise the hands and arms in the air and increase the speed of the pattern).

SIMPLE SCHOOLED FIGURES

Simple schooled figures are those figures in which the ability to float and/or to perform simple propulsion are required. These figures have a low difficulty rating (from 1.1 through 1.4) and are fun for the beginning synchronized class. A complete description of the simple figures may be found in the *Official Synchronized Swimming Handbook* of the Amateur Athletic Union.

SUMMARY

1. Fundamental skills in synchronized swimming are breathing and breath holding, floating, propulsion sculling, scooping and pulling, modified standard swimming strokes, egg-beater kick, and simple schooled figures.

2. The development of propulsion sculling paves the way to more difficult motor skills in synchronized swimming.

3. Modified standard swimming strokes are a prerequisite for the sport of synchronized swimming.

4. Simple schooled figures are those with a difficulty rating from 1.1 through 1.4.

3

STABLE POSITIONS:
BASE, DERIVATIONS,
AND DIFFICULTY

Stable positions are those positions that are held relatively stationary in the water. Twenty-six different stable positions are identified in this chapter. These positions, which are balanced by muscle tension and supported by sculling in the relative plane and depth of the body position, are subject to buoyancy and the force of gravity.

The authors have taken license to establish three distinct groups of stable positions: *horizontal, vertical,* and *axial*. Within each group there exists a learning progression made possible by the close relationship between the base position and the derivations to the base. The name of the base position is also part of the name given to other positions that are related. Each group derives its name from the general position of the trunk and head in relation to the water surface. *Horizontal* (or nearly so) and *vertical* are self-explanatory. Axial is a new term that refers to those positions of flexion or hyperextension of the trunk and head. The trunk and head are not horizontal or vertical; nor are they truly extended. They are so positioned to create a circular line, either concave or convex. Because axial skeleton is a descriptive term used in anatomy with reference to the head and torso, we have taken license in our use of this word to identify a group of stable positions that are homogeneous in head and torso alignment.

From our experience, we suggest teaching the stable positions beginning with the least difficult position listed in the horizontal group and progressing through the derivations in numerical order. For teaching purposes, each position has been assigned an approximate difficulty on a scale from one-tenth to six-tenths, simple to difficult. The degree of difficulty is listed after each position (see Appendix A). Then, follow with the axial positions and conclude with the vertical positions. We have found that this procedure not only fosters rapid association between the name and the corresponding body position but also enhances continuity from one lesson to another and from one position to another.

With few exceptions, each stable position may be taught in shallow water. Although standing, walking, or placing the hands on the pool floor may cause loss of points for the competitor, in a pool classroom situation great gain is derived from using the pool floor, wall, and trough as fixed apparatus for the learning and practice of stable positions. When holding the trough, it is possible to position the body in nearly all the vertical stable positions listed in this chapter. By placing the hands on the pool floor, the swimmer may develop the feeling for the tuck vertical (legs flexed, torso vertical), bent knee vertical (legs flexed only at the knee, thighs and torso vertical), split axial (legs split apart, pelvis tilted forward, upper torso vertical), and split axial variant (torso and one leg hyperextended, one leg flexed). The front pike vertical and front pike variant require the use of the pool wall and the trough. (See Stable Positions, Plates 1–25.)

Because support sculling at the hips (top depth) must accompany the teaching of the horizontal group of stable positions, it is the fundamental skill to emphasize in early lesson plans. Following shallow-water practice of each base and the derivations, the teacher should explain the arm patterns used for support and the sculling depths that correspond with each position. (Refer to chapter 4 for support sculling transitions and sculling depths.)

We suggest that the synchronized swimmer make use (similar to the gymnast's use of fixed apparatus) of the shallow water, trough, and wall. This phase of learning is identified as *aqua gymnastics.*

In listing the derivations of the front and back layout positions, we have included those positions that are readily learned with and adaptable to the horizontal group although in some instances the torso line may be diagonal to the water surface. Therefore, for teaching purposes, although the torso is not horizontal but slightly diagonal, the open and closed back tuck axial positions appear as derivations of the horizontal group. The same procedure has been followed in the listing of the front tuck position. Likewise, the back pike variant is shown as a derivation of the vertical group although the torso is diagonal to the water surface.

The basic concept of this chapter is to begin by teaching the stable position, base, and derivations, then follow with support sculling before the swimmer is asked to execute the schooled figure transitions. Once the swimmer has learned to balance and support the stable positions, movement between these positions will become more readily controlled.

Just as chapter 3, "Stable Positions," purposely follows "Developing Fundamental Skills," so "Arm Patterns" succeeds "Stable Positions," representing the teaching progressions recommended by the authors.

The following pictures clearly show the body line and the support sculling depth that correspond with the stable position. For display purposes in the classroom, an enlarged chart of the stable positions is available from Champions on Film, of Ann Arbor, Michigan. Twelve synchronized swimming loop films relative to this text are also available from them.

STABLE POSITIONS

HORIZONTAL GROUP

Base

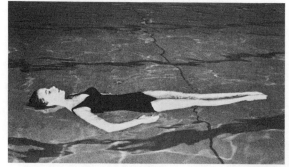

PLATE 1
Back Layout   .1*

Derivations of the Base

PLATE 2
Back Layout, variant   .2*

(a) open   PLATE 3   (b) closed
** Back Tuck   .1*

Base

Derivations of the Base

PLATE 4
Front Layout .1*

PLATE 5
Front Layout, variant .2*

PLATE 6
** Front Tuck .2*

PLATE 7
Ballet Leg, single .3*

PLATE 8
Ballet Leg, single variant .4*

PLATE 9
Ballet Legs, double .5*

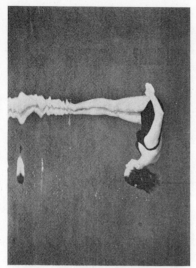

PLATE 10
Ballet Leg Submarine, single   .3*

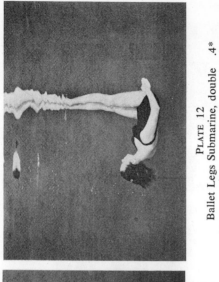

PLATE 11
Ballet Leg Submarine, single variant   .3*

PLATE 12
Ballet Legs Submarine, double   .4*

VERTICAL GROUP

Base

PLATE 13
Vertical, low water line   .3*

Derivations of the Base

PLATE 14
Vertical, tuck   .3*

PLATE 15
Vertical, bent knee   .2*

27

PLATE 16
Vertical, front pike .4*

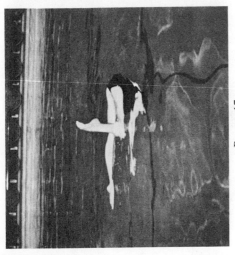

PLATE 17
Vertical, front pike variant .3*

PLATE 18
** Axial, back pike variant .3*

PLATE 19
Vertical, high water line .6*

PLATE 20
Vertical, variant .4*

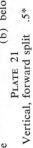

(a) surface (b) below the surface
PLATE 21
Vertical, forward split .5*

AXIAL GROUP

Base

PLATE 22
Axial, split .4*

(a) surface

(b) below the surface

Derivations of the Base

PLATE 23
Axial, split variant .5*

(a) surface

(b) below the surface

PLATE 24
Axial, reverse split .6*

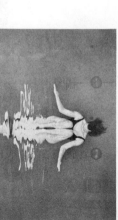

(a) surface

(b) below the surface

PLATE 25
Axial, tuck tip up .3*

(a) surface

(b) below the surface

* Indicates degree of difficulty.
** An axial position that is taught with the vertical positions.

29

In this chapter several names of stable positions are unique and original. Also many positions are original. To assist the reader in understanding the new nomenclature given to established positions that appear in the *AAU Synchronized Swimming Handbook,* a listing of positions with multiple names is offered.

Name	*Position*
Axial, back tuck open	Tub
Axial, back tuck closed	Tuck
Vertical, forward split	Fishtail or Crane
Axial, tuck tip up	Kip
Vertical, variant	Heron
Ballet Leg, single variant	Flamingo
Front Layout, variant	Bent knee
Back Layout, variant	Bent knee
Axial, reverse split	Knight

SUMMARY

1. Stable positions are those positions that are held static and balanced and remain relatively stationary in the water.
2. Stable positions are recognized as either horizontal, vertical, or axial and belong to one of these groups.
3. A variety of stable positions share a common base position.
4. Stable positions are assigned a difficulty rating from one-tenth to six-tenths, simple to complex.
5. The teaching of stable positions begins with the base position and progresses through the derivatives of the base.

4

ARM PATTERNS:
PROPULSION AND SUPPORT

The synchronized swimmer is a unique specialist in the art of using the arms for support of weight, for establishing equilibrium, and for propelling the body along a horizontal, vertical, or diagonal line. Because these skills are integral parts of each competitive figure, the swimmer must work long hours to develop strength, perfect timing, know the amount of force to apply, and show good efficiency in all the arm patterns. (*Efficiency* here refers to the ratio between the amount of work accomplished and the force or energy expended.) Good efficiency is top quality performance accompanied with effortlessness.

Through a variety of movements afforded the swimmer by the shoulder girdle, the elbow, and the wrist, a dynamic force range is available. At one extreme, there is force enough to drive the vertical body into the air feet-first until the water line is near the waist. At the opposite extreme, the swimmer may exert a diminutive force with the hands that is nearly equal to the delicate surface tension of the water.

PROPULSION: PRIMARY AND SECONDARY

In the schooled figure performance, with the exception of three possible *secondary forces* (i.e., gravity, buoyancy, and a body press), propulsion is the result of three *primary forces* (sculling, scooping, and pulling). See chapter 2

for a description of each. Through the use of primary propulsion, it is possible
to drive the body upward, downward, forward, and backward, as well as to
revolve it around a body axis. During the propulsion phase of a schooled figure,
or a part of a figure, in which the body revolves around a fixed point located
either within or outside the body, the arms provide the primary driving force.
The direction of the force will result in moving the body opposite to that force
direction. (An exception: when horizontal, opposing sculling forces serve to
drive the body around its dorso-ventral axis.) Examples of the most common
propulsion techniques follow. Somersaults are propelled by a combination of
scoops and pulls timed with the position of the moving body during its revolu-
tion. The dolphin circle is propelled by overhead sculling in a headfirst direction
until the body has rotated about the shoulders, at which time sculling headfirst
continues at the hips, driving the body upward and backward. (The dolphin may
be considered by some as an archaic remnant from the water ballet era.) Its
execution seldom, if ever, corresponds with its description in the AAU handbook. A foot-first dolphin is propelled by sculling feet first at the hips, followed
by strong lateral scoops. The intent is to move the body an equal distance
around a fixed point, the apex of the circle, until the back layout is assumed.
Sculling overhead headfirst concludes the schooled figure.

A twist is propelled by a modified sculling pattern with the hands above the
head or with the forearms and hands at chest depth. A twist of 180 or 360
degrees may be executed in a vertical high water line or a vertical low water line.
The vertical high water line twist is supported and propelled by the arms sculling
at mid depth, whereas the low water line twist is executed with the arms at
bottom depth.

A spin of 360 or 180 degrees is propelled by an inward press of one
arm moving toward the mid-body line with the wrist extended, the opposite
forearm is pressed above the head, rotated outward, and pressed to the back in
that order. A spin begins at vertical high water line and concludes before the heels
sink below the surface.

To assist the swimmer in understanding primary propulsion, it is helpful
to know that the arm is composed of three levers: the upper arm, forearm, and
hand. All primary propulsion techniques should be associated with the lever
or levers involved in the movement. When the performer of schooled figures
is learning to use these levers to control her movements, the pattern of action
may be referred to as a pull, scoop, or propulsion sculling. These have been
previously described. Our concern here is the identification of a half scoop or
half pull. Because only part of the arm is directly involved in the movement
(forearm and hand), the action is one created by a short lever. The upper arm
is held relatively stationary as the forearm is rotated outward and flexed during
the half scoop, or rotated inward and extended during the half pull. The movement is primarily around the point located in the elbow (fulcrum) as the
forearm and hand press against the water. To simplify what may appear to be a
maze of propulsion patterns, the swimmer should be able to recognize and

execute *rotation* of the levers of the arm. Rotation is the small twisting movement of a lever about its longitudinal axis. Also important is the technique referred to as a *recovery*. The recovery is a movement of one or more levers of the arm through the water in a line of least resistance to a point of greater mechanical advantage.

When the teacher-coach is giving emphasis to good timing and the use of propulsion to move the body a given specified distance, *range of motion* should be explained. The length of the lever in the propulsive pattern is important here. The space taken in or covered by the arm pattern is the range of motion involved in the propulsion. For example, the range of a scoop is increased to its maximum by extending the forearm and hand, locking the elbow and wrist joints so that the total arm may be moved as one lever from the shoulder. Accordingly, the range of motion may be decreased by flexing the elbow and wrist to bring the hand close to the body. A vivid example of the use of range of motion is readily recognized in the figure transition from a front layout to a front pike vertical. For the most effective use of range for this transition, place the arms below the shoulders and scull outward. A modified sculling headfirst permits the greatest efficiency in overcoming inertia and setting the body in motion at a speed that can be controlled without the torso overshooting the front pike vertical. A chest press downward is controlled by a series of half pulls that widen out from the body to a full pull as the torso rotates around the shoulders and slips into the vertical.

When the terms used to describe the possible propulsion patterns are familiar to the swimmer and each pattern can be executed, the labyrinth of propulsive techniques will become a clearly recognizable and describable sequence of action. The teacher-coach should be able to demonstrate on deck the following propulsive patterns: pull, scoop, half pull, half scoop, rotation, recovery, and range of motion. The following chart on propulsion includes a movement analysis of the levers of the arms during propulsion sculling, pulling, scooping, twisting, and spinning. The approximate range of action representative of good mechanical advantage for the corresponding body position is also described. "Propulsion at a Glance" may be used as a checklist against the swimmers' performances. Be sure each swimmer learns to propel all the body positions listed in the left column.

Arm Positions used for Propulsion

The inverted modified **L** is an arm position related to figures in the vertical group that have a water line from ankle to mid calf. The upper arms are abducted until in line with the shoulders. The forearms are flexed until vertical. The wrists are hyperextended. This position is used to propel low water line twists (see bottom depth sculling, Figure 22).

The inverted **T** is an arm position used to propel various high water line vertical positions. Because it is most effective in the support of airborne weight,

CHART I

ANALYSIS OF MOVEMENT OF THE LEVERS OF THE ARM PROPULSION AT A GLANCE

Body position	General position of the arms to begin	Direction of pressure	Direction of travel	Position and action of upper arms	Action of forearms	Position and action of the hands
Standard scull, back layout	Arms at side of torso; shoulder girdle stationary	Toward feet	Toward head	45° or less between arm and torso	Inward rotation as forearms extend; outward rotation as they flex	Wrists hyperextended; hands slightly abduct as forearms extend; adduct as forearms are flexed
Reverse standard scull, back layout	Same as above	Toward head	Toward feet	Same as above	Same as above	Maximum flexion of wrists as forearms rotate
Propeller scull, back layout	Arms outstretched beyond head; shoulders elevated	Away from head	Toward feet	Near side of head and held stationary	Same as above	Wrists hyperextended; abduction of hands as forearms extend; adduction of hands as forearms flex
Reverse propeller scull, back layout	Arms outstretched beyond head; shoulders elevated	Toward feet	Toward head	Near side of head and held stationary	Inward rotation with extension and outward rotation with flexion	Wrists flexed; abduction of hands as forearms extend; adduction as forearms flex

Standard scull, front layout	At side of body	Toward feet	Toward head	Hyperextended; held at approximately 45° between arm and torso	Inward rotation extension and outward rotation with flexion	Wrists extended; abduction of hands as forearms extend; adduction as forearms flex
Propeller scull, front layout	Arms outstretched beyond head; shoulders elevated	Away from head	Toward feet	Near side of head and held stationary	Same as above	Wrists hyperextended; abduction of hands as forearms extend; adduction as forearms flex
Back tuck, open or closed (turning on dorso-ventral axis)	Arms at side of body; shoulder girdle stationary	Toward head with one hand; toward feet with other hand	Rotates around dorso-ventral axis	Held at approximately 45° between arm and torso	Same as above	One wrist hyperextended, one wrist flexed; abduction and adduction with forearm rotation as here-to-fore described
Vertical, twist scull (head downward slowly)	Inverted modified L	Toward head as left hand moves inward; away from head as right hand moves outward	Rotates around longitudinal axis slowly	Abducted to shoulder level and held stationary	Flexion followed by extension in inward and outward rotation; forearms begin in vertical position	Hyperextended

CHART I Continued

Body position	General position of the arms to begin	Direction of travel	Direction of pressure	Position and action of upper arms	Action of forearms	Position and action of the hands
No. 1 Vertical, 180° spin press	Inverted **T**	Rotates around longitudinal axis	Toward front of body as left upper arm adducts; toward pool floor as right upper arm abducts	1. Left upper arm pressed through horizontal extension and adduction 2. To complete pattern, left upper arm rotated inward and abducted until over head 1. Right upper arm abducts until over head	1. With left thumb facing pool floor, left forearm flexed and pressed toward front of body until arc of approximately 180° completed 2. Left forearm then rotated inward and extended toward pool floor 1. Right forearm flexed as it moves toward head; rotate inward and extend over head	1. Left hand extended during arc of 180°; hyperextended as left forearm extended over head; right hand hyperextended throughout pattern
Vertical, 360° spin press	Inverted **T**	Rotates around longitudinal axis	Toward front of body as left upper arm adducts; toward pool floor as right upper arm abducts	Same as listed in no. 1 description for both left and right upper arms	Same as listed in no. 1 description for both left and right forearms	Left hand extended and right hand hyperextended

Vertical, high water line slow twist	Inverted T	Downward toward pool floor and outward from longitudinal line of body	Rotates around longitudinal axis	1. Upper arms slightly abducted at lateral body line 2. Forearms move through adduction with outward rotation 3. Recovery consists of abduction and inward rotation	1. Flexed and forcefully rotated outward Forearms swing to side of body over range of approximately 80° 2. Forceful outward rotation released on inward swing	Palms held supinated throughout, facing pool floor
Pull, front layout	Arms outstretched beyond head	Toward feet	Toward head	1. Slight inward rotation 2. Adducted along a horizontal line during pull	Rotated inward	Extends in line with forearms
Pull, back layout	Same as above	Same as above	Same as above	Same as above	Same as above	Same as above
Scoop, front layout	Arms outstretched along side of body	Toward head	Toward feet	Rotated outward on scoop, upper arms are abducted above the head	Outward rotation and extension	Extended in line with forearm
Scoop, back layout	Same as above	Same as above	Same as above	Rotated outward and abducted during scoop	Same as above	Wrists in line with forearms

it is used at the height of thrusting figures, just prior to a spin, or to propel a slow twist with maximum sustained height. The inverted **T** has greatest mechanical advantage when the upper arms are abducted (placed nearly parallel to the vertical torso with elbows near hips), the elbows being flexed, and the hands in an extended position. The hands are parallel to the water surface, with the palms facing the pool floor. When the inverted **T** position is increased in range by abducting the upper arms and moving the forearms a greater distance away from the lateral body line, the mechanical advantage is weakened. However, an increase in range favors the speed of the hands through the water, a desirable and necessary technique for the propulsion of a spin (figure 17).

The feather press is a modified scoop that weaves toward the head along the lateral body line when the torso is vertical. Its use will drive the body from a low water line to one of maximum height. In the figure performance it is used to momentarily stabilize and support a high water line just prior to a vertical descent. It may begin at any range position of the arms shown in the inverted **T** (see mid depth sculling, Figure 21).

The spin-press arm pattern propels the body around its longitudinal axis. From a full-range inverted **T** position, one arm rapidly presses toward the front of the mid body line to set the body in motion. The opposite arm executes a lateral scoop. Note: It is possible to execute a spin of 180° without a noticeable

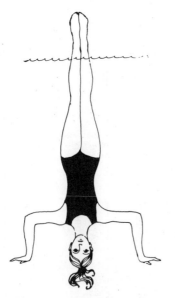

FIG. 16   Inverted modified **L**

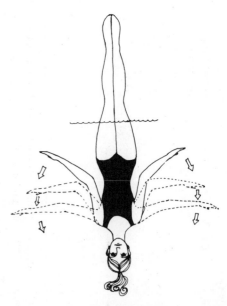

FIG. 17   Inverted **T**

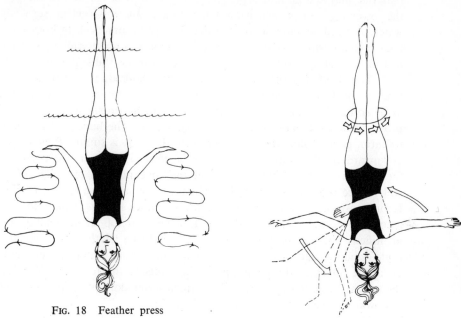

FIG. 18   Feather press

FIG. 19   Spin press

drop in height. This is accomplished by shortening the mid body press so that
the arms may be used to support scull the airborne weight of the legs.

Secondary propulsion is the biomechanics of the legs, trunk, chest, head,
the forces of gravity, and buoyancy. In the air or water, the levers of the legs
are moved by flexion, extension, adduction, abduction, and rotation inward or
outward. The toes are plantar flexed. The flexible nature of the spine permits
isolated movement of the chest. It is curled forward, uncurled or laterally flexed
when moving from horizontal to vertical, or vice versa. The trunk, as one lever,
moves against the water resistance by flexion, extension, hyperextension, and
lateral rotation. Gravity assists the descent of a body lever, whereas buoyancy
aids the ascent. Chapter V presents examples of these biomechanics.

SUPPORT

Perhaps the greatest objective for the synchronized swimmer is to develop
the skill to support airborne weight and balance it so that movement may occur
around a fixed point within the body (center of gravity or center of pelvis)
while keeping that point relatively stationary. Good support techniques should
enhance stability when such techniques are combined with good alignment of
body parts. Support techniques are designed to control and combat the force
of gravity and to support weight. Because a beginning synchronized swimmer
cannot be expected to support airborne weight, two of the support sculling

patterns, mid and bottom depth, may be practiced at the wall of the pool where the lower legs are pressed against the deck as the torso hangs vertically in the water. A third sculling depth, top depth, may be practiced in both the front or back layout positions. For rapid understanding of support sculling we have identified three sculling depths used to support the various stable positions of the body.

Top depth support sculling occurs while the body is horizontal in either the front or back layout. Support is the result of forearm rotation about the elbow as flexion and extension occur. The hands are hyperextended when the body is prone so that the palms may face the pool floor. The hands are in line with the forearm, palms facing the pool floor when the body is supine. Pressure is exerted downward on the water during both the inward and outward rotary phase of the forearm. The uplifting force near the concentration of weight of the body will reduce other muscular forces that are necessary to maintain the horizontal layout position. The uplift will aid the swimmer in her attempt to stretch out along the desirable horizontal line. Efficiency in top depth sculling is readily identified. The size of the pattern is less than the width of the shoulders. It is rapid, smooth, and constant in speed. As the wrists slightly adduct and abduct (whip of fingers) whirlpools appear just outside the forearms. Whirlpools tell the coach the action is sucking the surface water downward instead of churning it upward, a sign of undesirable turbulence.

In the drawings that follow, each sculling depth described has an area (range) identified by a shaded geometric shape. The width of the area represents the inward and outward sculling movement, whereas the depth represents the approximate down press of the lever involved in the movement.

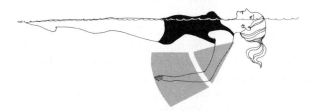

FIG. 20   Top depth support sculling

A second sculling depth is identified as *mid depth*. The vertical group of stable positions, with few exceptions, require support at mid depth from the front to near the lateral line of the body. This movement pattern is difficult to learn because the forearm is very seldom held in a position of extreme outward rotation (turning the thumbs outward as the hand supinates). Whirlpools are not created at the surface as described in top depth sculling. The distinguishing feature in mid depth sculling is the position and action of the upper arm. This lever is held nearly vertical to the surface and slightly abducts and adducts about the lateral line of the body. It is forcefully rotated outward at the shoulder as the forearm swings through a range of forty-five to eighty degrees. The elbow is flexed until the forearm is nearly parallel to the water surface (Figure 21).

A third support sculling depth is referred to as *bottom depth*. Some specific stable positions from the vertical and axial groups require support at this depth. (See the support sculling chart on page 48.) To identify the correct position corresponding to bottom depth sculling, the upper arms must be abducted along the lateral line of the body until the elbows are level with or slightly above the shoulders. The forearms remain flexed at the elbow and become the vertical portion of the lever. The wrists are hyperextended so that the hand may remain behind the forearm during flexion, extension, and rotation of that lever. The effective sculling range of movement is approximately ten inches in width.

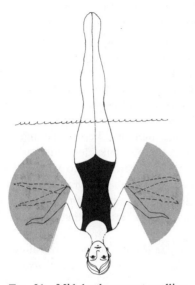

FIG. 21   Mid depth support sculling

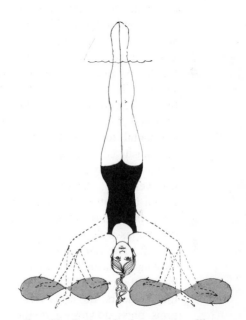

FIG. 22   Bottom depth support sculling

It is helpful to know that for training purposes both propulsion and support patterns of the arms may be repeated over and over during practice without undue fatigue. Propulsion or support by the legs alone expends energy two to four times greater than comparable arm movements.[1]

Having described the anatomical movements used in support sculling at three distinct depths, we will now describe a sequence of supportive patterns that connect one sculling depth to another. Support sequences are used by the synchronized swimmer during the flow of torso and leg movements in

[1] Faulkner, John A. *What Research Tells the Coach About Swimming.* Washington, D.C.: Library of Congress, 1967. Catalog card no. 67–24087. Printed for the American Association for Health, Physical Education, and Recreation, 1201 16th St., N.W., Washington, D.C.

competitive figures. The sculling depth and range of movement change to correspond with the relocation and balance of the weight of the body parts. Such a sequence is referred to as a "support transition." Two distinct support transitions are effective in figure control. Each follows a sequence that enables the swimmer to move the hands and arms to a point of greater mechanical advantage while keeping constant pressure on the water.

1. The *scull, recovery, catch, and scull* transition is used when moving the arms from top depth to mid depth or from bottom depth to mid depth. The recovery phase in this transition is a brief release of pressure during which time the arms rotate outward and flex at the elbow. When moving the torso from horizontal to a vertical variant or forward split, the recovery is most effective in controlling the distribution of leg weight when it occurs following the inward sweep of the sculling pattern. While moving in a line of least resistance, the inward recovery requires the least amount of time to arrive at the point where a *catch* of good mechanical advantage is to be executed under the center of the weight. The catch is a significant part of this support sequence as it establishes the proper angle of the hand to the water through which uplifting force is achieved. This support transition is highly effective when pressing the torso from horizontal to vertical variant, as in the flamingo bent knee figure, or when pressing from vertical low water line to double ballet legs submarine, as in the hightower. However, when a high water line vertical is to be established (both legs vertical), the recovery and catch are made following the outward sweep of the forearm during top depth sculling. This enables the swimmer to quickly place the hands along the lateral body line, a position that will assist the body balance as well as support it.

2. The *scull, lateral feather press, scull* is a support transition used when moving the arms from mid depth to bottom depth. The lateral *feather press* is a modified scoop. The arms are elevated during the feather press to a point above the shoulders, the arms weave from front to back of the lateral body line as the arms press downward in the water.

These two support transitions may be practiced at the wall of the pool. The lower legs are flexed at the knee and pressed across the deck to anchor and stabilize the body so that the support transitions may be coordinated with the torso press from horizontal to vertical and returned to horizontal.

Schooled figure transitions that revolve around a fixed point within the body are subject to the strong vertical force of gravity. To gain maximum control over this force, the coach and swimmer must understand the simple principles of leverage. For example, when sculling at top depth, maximum support is the result of sculling near the hips along the lateral line of the body, using the forearm and hand as the resistance arm, the elbow as the fulcrum. The fulcrum is the center of the joint around which a lever moves. When the elbow is moved outward from the lateral body line and the resistance force (hand) is moved a greater distance from the hips (fixed point), the uplifting force is decreased because the increase in range represents a position of less mechanical advantage.

The lateral feather press is an excellent example of maximum range within a support transition. The fulcrum is located within the shoulder girdle. The resistance arm is a single shaft from the shoulder to the finger tip. This lever rotates about the shoulder girdle. Unfortunately, such an arrangement favors speed of movement at the expense of force. Therefore, the lateral press must be feathered to increase the time required to partially support the airborne weight, a desirable characteristic in the figure execution that assists constant speed of action.

Support sculling transitions must be properly timed with the movement of other body parts so that weight is supported and balance is achieved. When the support transition is poorly timed with the movement of the torso or legs, loss of height and traveling off the fixed point will result. (Poorly timed support transitions are either too early or too late for the change in body line.) A poorly timed support transition is readily identified when the swimmer attempts to save a transition by contracting muscles that will cause a loss of equalized forces responsible for good body alignment.

Without question the greatest advance in competitive figure performance has been the result of teaching the swimmer to support scull in the area close to the center of gravity, or fixed point within the body position and in line with it. When the most efficient support transition is used, regardless of the weight and height of the swimmer, greater elevation, balance, and timing will be achieved. By placing the resistance arm in the area of greatest mechanical advantage, figure control will be improved.

The chart, "Support at a Glance," should be used as a checklist against the swimmer's ability to support all the stable positions listed in the left column.

CHART II

Analysis of Movement of the Levers of the Arm Support at a Glance

Body position	General position of the arms to begin	Direction of pressure	Position and action of upper arms	Action of forearms	Position and action of the hands
Back layout Back layout variant** Back tuck open** closed	Along side of body; shoulder girdle stationary	Toward pool floor	Abducted and held at a 45° angle or less to the torso	Slight inward rotation with forearm extension; outward rotation with forearm flexion	Wrists extended, palms flat, fingers firmly together; abduction and adduction
Ballet leg, single Ballet leg, single variant** Ballet legs, double	Same as above	Toward pool floor with increased speed	Same as above	Same as above Deepened in the water to remain in line with center of gravity of body	Same as above
Ballet leg submarine, single*	At side of body with elbows flexed	To remain at ankle depth			

*Stable positions not identified in the AAU synchronized swimming handbook

**Identified in the handbook by another name

Ballet leg submarine, single variant*	1. Toward pool floor	Held at side of torso	Outward rotation with flexion; inward rotation with flexion	Extension of forearm; palms flat, fingers firm
Ballet legs submarine, double*	2. Toward surface and head—a half scoop	Outward rotation with adduction	Maximum outward rotation with flexion (scoop)	Moves with forearm as one lever
	3. Careful recovery to hips	Inward rotation and abduction	Inward rotation and extension	Slices with little resistance
Front layout Front layout variant Front tuck	Along sides of torso	Hyperextended and held at approximately 45° or more to torso	Inward rotation with extension; outward rotation with flexion	Wrists hyperextended; abduction of hands as forearms extend; adduction as forearms flex
Vertical, front pike**	Arms outstretched in front of body, reaching to align with center of gravity; hands between surface and waistline depth Inverted **T**	Toward pool floor and outward from center line of body	Outward rotation, adduction, and flexion, followed by abduction and inward rotation	Some flexion and held at maximum outward rotation during sculling pattern
Front pike variant*	Same as above	Same as above	Outward rotation with adduction; inward rotation with abduction	Flexion and held at maximum outward rotation during support pattern	Same as above

45

CHART II *Continued*

Body position	General position of the arms to begin	Direction of pressure	Position and action of upper arms	Action of forearms	Position and action of the hands
Vertical, low water line (ankle to mid calf)	Inverted modified **L**	Diagonal toward pool floor	Abducted until in line with shoulders; held slightly to front of torso	Flexed to 90° to begin; inward rotation with extension; outward rotation with flexion	Wrists hyperextended
Vertical, high water line	Inverted **T**	Toward pool floor and outward from center line of body	Outward rotation with adduction; inward rotation with abduction	Flexion and held at maximum outward rotation during support pattern	Wrists extended; traverses approximately 80°
Vertical variant*	Inverted **T**	Toward pool floor and outward from center line of body	Outward rotation with adduction; inward rotation with abduction	Flexion and held at maximum outward rotation during support pattern	Wrists extended; Traverses approximately 80°
Vertical, forward split** (knee to hip water line)	Same as above	Same as above	Same as above	Same as above	Same as above

	L or inverted T	Same as above	Same as vertical with high water line		
Axial, reverse split		Same position and action as described in vertical with high water line			Kept near lateral line of body
Axial, split variant*	Above head; full range of inverted modified L	Toward pool floor	Abducted above shoulder line and held stationary	Flexed and extended; inward rotation with extension and outward rotation with flexion	Wrists hyperextended
Axial, tuck*	Inverted T	Toward pool floor with limited down press	Nearly vertical along side of torso; adduction and outward rotation followed by abduction and inward rotation	Flexed and held at maximum outward rotation followed by extension in rotated position	Slowly moving with forearm as an extension of that lever; hands traverse a range of approximately 45°
Vertical, tuck*	Inverted T	Toward pool floor with limited down press	Nearly vertical along side of torso; adduction and outward rotation	Flexed and held at maximum outward rotation, followed by extension in rotated positions	Extended as continuation of forearms; hands swing to lateral line of body
Vertical, bent knee*	Inverted modified L	Same as vertical with low water line			

SCULLING DEPTHS FOR HORIZONTAL, VERTICAL,
AND AXIAL GROUPS OF STABLE POSITIONS

Horizontal Group   *Top depth*

    Front layout
    Front layout, variant
    Front tuck
    Back layout
    Back layout, variant
    Back tuck open and closed
    Ballet leg, single
    Ballet leg, single variant
    Ballet legs, double
    Ballet leg submarine, single
    Ballet leg submarine, single variant
    Ballet legs submarine, double

Vertical Group   *Mid depth*

    Vertical, tuck
    Vertical, bent knee   Exception: *Bottom depth*
    Vertical, low water line   Exception: *Bottom depth*
    Vertical, front pike
    Vertical, front pike variant
    Vertical, variant
    Vertical, high water line
    Vertical, forward split

Axial Group   *Bottom depth*

    Axial, split
    Axial, split variant
    Axial, reverse split   Exception: *Mid depth*
    Axial, tuck tip up   Exception: *Mid depth*
    Axial, front pike variant

SUMMARY

1. Through movement patterns of the arms, the body is either propulsed or supported. These movements are sculling, scooping, or pulling.
2. Sculling provides a constant force against the water.

3. Both the scoop and the pull provide an intermittent force against the water because each has a recovery stage.

4. When body surfaces are elevated above the water surface, support sculling is required to maintain the position.

5. Support sculling at top, mid, or bottom depths must be related to, and appropriate for, support of each stable position.

6. The arm is divided into three levers. Each is analyzed for specific movement patterns.

5

SCHOOLED FIGURE TRANSITIONS

The outstanding feature of synchronized swimming that makes this activity a competitive sport is the schooled figure event. Since the late nineteen fifties, coaches and swimmers alike have experimented with techniques to find better control of transitional movement and greater height on stable positions. Today the national winner of the figure event represents an in-depth coaching master-piece as well as a dedicated and talented swimmer. In any level of competition the figure winner holds a covetous position that motivates other synchronized swimmers.

This chapter contains the essential information needed when coaching competitive figures or teaching the components of a figure. The descriptions relate the actual movement of groups of muscles and other parts of the body. The sequential pictures show the results of these movements. In an effort to further the knowledge about transitions, these movements have been refined according to the elements and basic characteristics contained within them. Those of like qualities have been grouped together to assist the teacher-coach in a classroom situation.

In figure performance, a movement that results in changing the swimmer's position in the water from a stable position to another, or returns the swimmer to the original starting position, is referred to as a figure transition. These movements involve the head, shoulders, chest, arms, spine, pelvis, and legs.

Each group of transitional movements has been identified according to the predominant elements present within the movement. For example, group one consists of stable or static positions that are propelled by scoops, pulls, propulsion sculling, or a simple body press. These positions revolve around a fixed point and a body axis. Included in this group are:

1. The horizontal roll (log roll, corkscrew)
2. The vertical twist, spins, and twisting in the forward split vertical
3. The surface circle (shark)
4. The tucked circle (somersaults)
5. The piked circle (somersaults)
6. The arched circle (dolphins and swordfish)
7. The circle of decreasing circumference (tailspin)

The distinguishing element in group one is propulsion of a near static position.

Group two represents airborne movement of the legs, during which the torso is aligned horizontally or vertically in the water. Examples are:

1. The front pike vertical to vertical (porpoise transition)
2. The front pike vertical to the split axial (walkover front transition)
3. The front pike vertical to vertical variant (albatross transition)
4. All ballet leg transitions

The predominant elements present in group two are support sculling at top depth or mid depth during airborne leg movements.

Group three may be referred to as gravity transitions. This group includes the submarine movements. Propulsion is provided by the force of gravity and a scoop during the holding of the stable position.

With few exceptions, the remaining transitions become triplex because three forms of movement are present. One of two possible sequences describe the triplex transition: propulsion by the arms, followed by a body press, followed by support sculling (PBS); or support sculling, followed by a body press, followed by support sculling (SBS). These triplex transitions are referred to as PBS and SBS. Examples of PBS are:

1. Movement from the front layout to the front pike vertical (porpoise transition)
2. Movement from the back layout to the front pike vertical (albatross transition)
3. Movement from the back layout to a high water line vertical (spiral transition)

(There is controversy over which element comes first, arm propulsion or body press, in some specific transitions.)

Examples of SBS are:

1. Movement from the single ballet leg to the forward split vertical (catalina transition)
2. Movement from the forward split vertical to the submarine single ballet leg (reverse catalina transition)
3. Movement from double ballet legs to the vertical (flamingo transition)
4. Movement from the single ballet leg variant to vertical variant (flamingo bent knee transition)
5. Movement from the single ballet leg to the reverse split axial (castle transition)

With few exceptions, each transition in this chapter belongs to one of the movement groups previously described. Therefore, we recommend that both teacher and swimmer be able to recognize the basic movements used in each movement sequence and identify the group to which the transition belongs. Such an in-depth analysis will clarify and simplify what at first may appear to be a complex labyrinth of movement.

An understanding by the swimmer of the sequence of movements within a transition nurtures neuromuscular control of the movement. For example: basically, the flamingo transition from double ballet legs to high water line vertical is an SBS transition. The sequence of movement begins by support sculling at top depth near the hips, followed by a down press of the shoulders to vertical. The arms recover to the mid depth, catch, and support scull. We believe this type of movement analysis is clear, concise, and readily understood. For the swimmer, however, understanding the movement fulfills only half the challenge, for when the body muscles involved in the movement are not strong enough to handle the load sent as a message from the nerves, extraneous movement will cause faults. When sculling is weak in this particular flamingo transition, the shoulder press to vertical is inhibited by unstable hips and legs. Therefore, to save the movement from near failure, the swimmer will pull the arms through the water, forcing the torso downward. By so doing, a primary propulsion technique is erroneously added to the prescribed sequence of movement. Because arm propulsion is not one of the basic movements in this transition, its use will result in the body traveling. SBS transitions are to be performed in a relatively stationary position around a fixed point within the hip area; therefore, propulsion by the arms must be excluded. The swimmer can easily feel this error and work to correct it.

Usage and application of this type of analysis is not limited to the teacher and swimmer. The judge of figures substantiates the given score by means of a similar appraisal of the several transitions combined to constitute a figure.

Within each group of transitions there exists progressive difficulty. For example, propulsion of a static tuck position is less difficult than propulsion of a static pike position. Because the tuck position minimizes resisting body surfaces, it is less difficult to propel than either the front or back pike positions in which resisting surfaces are at maximum.

Those transitions found in group two (airborne legs with the torso horizontal or vertical) become more difficult as greater weight is shifted from the water surface to the air. Hence, it is easier to execute a single ballet leg than double ballet legs; or, when beginning in a front pike position, it is easier to execute a forward split vertical than a high water line vertical.

PBS transitions progress in difficulty according to the complexity of torso movement, which ultimately affects primary and secondary propulsion. For example, it is easier to press the body and scull it from a front layout to a front pike position, as in a porpoise, than to press, rotate, and scull from a back layout to a front pike position, as in an albatross. Also, whenever airborne weight is added to PBS transitions, difficulty is increased. For example: the dolphin bent knee offers greater resistance to propulsion than the dolphin. Likewise, SBS transitions become more difficult as airborne weight is increased during the torso press. For example, it is easier to move from a single ballet leg variant, as in the flamingo bent knee, than to move from a double ballet legs position to a high water line, as in the flamingo.

All too frequently the subtle movements of the arms are de-emphasized or overlooked in favor of the dynamic actions of the legs and torso. Such a situation contributes primarily to poor control of figure transitions. The teacher and swimmer must readily understand that arm actions play an integral part in transitions, that the greatest challenge is to coordinate and time the change of sculling depths with the transfer of weight and the change of torso line in relation to the water surface. Also, when propulsion is employed, the speed of the body through the water must not adversely affect the swimmer's ability to balance weight. Jerkiness and splashing during transitions are undesirable.

The figure performer must be programmed to use all the available forces in proper sequence and at the strategic time. Those forces are: muscle strength used in a body press; uplift from support sculling; and propulsion force resulting from pulling, scooping, a feather press, sculling, gravity, and buoyancy. These forces play a major role in figure transitions. When the swimmer understands how to use them and has developed sufficient strength, the performance will be greatly improved.

In figure competition, it is well to remember that transitions should be performed slowly to allow the swimmer opportunity to use these forces in a controlled manner. Following each transition there must be time allowed to align the center of gravity of the position with the center of buoyancy, if the position lends itself to such alignment, or find balance by means of support sculling. In each instance, support sculling in one of the three corresponding depths previously described in chapter 4 provides stability for each stable position, whereas the use of a proper sculling transition will enhance its counterpart, the torso movement in a figure transition. The sequence of balance, shift of weight, and rebalance, is a delicate combination and must be slowly executed so as to assist the swimmer in decreasing the muscular tug of war that is ever present in figure transitions.

The figure performer must use these forces just previously mentioned in a manner that will produce the desired performance, comply with the requirements of good control—i.e., effortlessness, smooth action, elevation, good timing—and remain relatively stationary (movement around a fixed point).

The highly skilled synchronized swimmer has developed the science of movement used in this sport. A good performer uses only those muscles that truly generate the movement, while other muscles are counterbalancing, holding, stabilizing, or relaxing. During all movements the highly skilled performer is able to stretch without strain, demonstrating a great degree of flexibility of the body joints and extensor muscles.

To assist the reader in understanding the vocabulary used in this chapter to describe transitional movement, the following terms are defined. These terms should be used by the teacher when communicating with the swimmer. Words that vividly describe the transitional action expedite teaching and learning; it is helpful to associate one word with each totally different movement.

Press	Refers to the torso and/or legs exerting pressure against the water upward, downward, forward, backward, or sideward.
Turn	Refers to a left or right change of direction when in a horizontal position (for example, a marlin).
Rotate	Refers to a clockwise or counterclockwise movement of a body lever turning in a horizontal plane about a vertical axis or vice versa.
Twist or Spin	Represents movements of the body around its longitudinal axis, moving the axis with the body as one unit. A twist has an established waterline, whereas the spin has a changing waterline.
Tip	Refers to a position of the legs or the body when leaning

to the left or the right of the mid-body line. Anatomically, this is called lateral flexion.

Pull   Refers to an arm action in which pressure is exerted against the water moving from head toward the feet.

Scoop   Refers to an arm action opposite to the pull. Pressure begins at the hips and moves toward the head.

Pike   Refers to flexing the legs at the hip socket.

Arch   Refers to a backward-downward movement of the spine.

Pivot roll   Involves a torso twist with lateral flexion while pressing the torso from horizontal to vertical or vice versa. The legs also twist but remain in their relative position to the water surface.

Other vocabulary may be found in the glossary on page 258.

The descriptions of transitions in this chapter do not include the speed of the movements; nor do they identify the specific muscles causing the action in phases of the movement. We have tried to identify what we refer to as stress muscles; that is, those groups of muscles that can be identified from the action of body segments in relation to one another. For example, in describing the single ballet leg, we have said that the hip flexors draw the thigh to the perpendicular position prior to extension of the lower leg. We have not identified by name a specific hip flexor muscle that might be responsible for this action. We leave that kind of identification to the biomechanic experts in electromyography. Nor have we identified every subtle action possible in each transition, but have concentrated on identifying the most important muscle groups, stress muscles, in order to produce the most desirable performance of top-level skill.

To use this chapter with some degree of success, we suggest the reader look at the underwater pictures to identify the part or parts of the body that appear to have moved in the picture sequence. Identify the lever or levers involved in the movement. Associate the support sculling depth with each stable body position and visualize the transitional sculling path taken by the arms if not shown. When the sculling transition is one of propulsion while holding a static position, take note of the direction of the palms of the hands. Then read the description to augment what you have seen.

Although the strength and buoyancy of each swimmer, as well as her flexibility and proportions, will cause minor variations in control of these transitions, the pictures reveal the dependable and workable techniques that have produced quality execution. Although the descriptions that accompany the pictures are sophisticated, we hope they will be used in the common classroom.

TRANSITIONS

Pictures and Descriptions of Movement from One Stable Position to Another

Back Layout   to   Back Variant

Ballet Leg Transition no. 1

BASIC
ELEMENTS   Support sculling, airborne leg action

STABLE
POSITION   While support sculling at the top depth near the hips, the body is afloat
                on its back in a horizontal line at the water surface. The extensors of the
                head, located along the back of the neck and lower skull, hold the head
                in line with the shoulders. The shoulders are slightly retracted; the chest
                is broad and elevated; the legs, knees, and ankles are extended; the toes are
                plantar flexed (pressed toward the sole of the foot). The hips are held
                at the water surface by the hip extensors. The contraction of the lower
                abdominals counterbalances the pull of the hip extensors to stabilize the
                body position.

SMOOTH
MOVEMENT   *To move from back layout to the back variant, the hip flexors of one
                leg draw the thigh toward the chest until it is perpendicular to the water
                surface. The adductors of the moving leg hold the thigh close to the mid-
                line of the body.*

PLATE 26

a

b

c

Back Layout, Variant   to   Ballet Leg, Single

Single Ballet Leg Extension Transition

BASIC
ELEMENTS   Support sculling, airborne leg action

STABLE
POSITION   Support sculling is at the top depth, increased in speed to provide uplift for the weight of the airborne leg. The head remains in line with the shoulders. The pelvis is stablized by the counterbalance of the hip extensors and abdominal contraction. Some adduction of both legs keeps the thighs close to the mid line of the body. In schooled figures, the ankles are always extended and the toes are plantar flexed.

SMOOTH
MOVEMENT   *Elevation of the lower leg becomes a very isolated movement. The swimmer must think about moving only the knee joint. Because the hip joint and the knee joint are flexed by the same muscle, the swimmer must learn to use only the distal end of that muscle to raise the lower part of the leg and foot to vertical extension. While the lower leg is moving to vertical, the same muscle at the hip joint must keep the thigh from moving.*

57

PLATE 27

a   b

Ballet Leg, Single   to   Back Layout, Variant

Single Ballet Leg Recovery Transition

BASIC
ELEMENTS   Support sculling, airborne leg action

STABLE
POSITION   The body and one leg are nearly horizontal at the water surface. The oppo-
                    site leg is held vertical at a ninety-degree angle to the water surface. The
                    anatomical markings that determine the vertical line are the outside of the
                    little toe, the ankle bone (outer maleolus), the outside of the knee, and
                    the outside center of the hip. The hip extensors hold the horizontal leg
                    at the surface. The head is held in line with the shoulders as the chest is
                    pressed to the water surface. Support sculling is at the top depth, rapid,
                    near the hips, and in line with the center of gravity of the position. The
                    pelvis is stabilized by lower abdominal contraction, counterbalanced by the
                    pull of the hip extensors. Some adduction of both legs keeps the thighs
                    close to the midline of the body.

SMOOTH
MOVEMENT   *To move the ballet leg to the back variant position, the airborne foot is
                    lowered by the same muscles that kept it vertical. A gradual release of the
                    knee extensors will allow the force of gravity to move the foot to the water.
                    So that the hip joint may remain motionless, only the distal end is released.
                    To arrive at the variant position, the pelvis is pressed toward the surface
                    by the hip extensors.* Refer to plate 27b and 27a, in that order, to view the
                    ballet leg recovery transition.

Back Layout   to   Back Tuck (open)

Double Ballet Legs Transition

BASIC
ELEMENTS   Support sculling, leg action

STABLE
POSITION   The back layout position was described in ballet leg transition no. 1.

SMOOTH
MOVEMENT   *To move from the back layout position to the back tuck open, support sculling is slowly performed at the top depth. The hip flexors draw the thighs toward the chest. The legs are held firmly together by the adductors. As the thighs move toward the body, the hips are allowed to settle in the water until the thighs are perpendicular to the water surface, with the lower legs held at the surface by the extensors of the knees.* Refer to plate 26a for the back layout starting position.

PLATE 28

a   b

Back Tuck (open)   to   Ballet Legs, Double

Double Ballet Legs Extension Transition

BASIC
ELEMENTS   Support sculling, airborne leg action

STABLE
POSITION   The torso is held on an angle to the water surface. The hips are submerged; the head and shoulders are nearly horizontal at the surface. Sculling is at

top depth, near the hips, and relatively slow. The legs are held firmly together by the adductors. The lower legs and feet are held at the surface of
the water by the knee extensors.

SMOOTH
MOVEMENT   *The sculling speed is increased to provide uplift for the weight of the legs.*
The legs are raised to the vertical by contraction of the knee extensors. The
pelvis is stabilized by the counterbalance of the abdominals and the hip ex-
tensors.

PLATE 29

a

b

Back Tuck (open)   to   Back Tuck (closed)

Kip or Back Somersault Transition

BASIC
ELEMENTS   Support sculling, leg action

STABLE
POSITION   The back tuck open position was described in the double ballet legs extension transition.

SMOOTH
MOVEMENT   *Sculling is relatively slow at the top depth. To move from the back tuck*
open to the back tuck closed position, the hip flexors contract to pull the
thighs toward the chest. The knees flex only slightly, keeping the feet at
the water surface. The thighs move under and around the knees until the
hip joint is closed. The abdominals pull to create a rounding of the back
from the lower rib cage to the end of the spine. The hips will surface as
the thighs move around the knees. The head is flexed forward. Buoyancy
uplift will aid the support of this position.

PLATE 30

a

b

c

Back Tuck (closed)   to   Axial, Tuck (tip up)

Kip Tip Up Transition

BASIC
ELEMENTS   Support sculling, body press, support sculling

STABLE
POSITION   The back tuck closed position requires maximum flexion of the legs, contraction of the abdominals, slightly protracted shoulders, and a flexed head. The position is held at the water surface by buoyancy and top depth sculling.

SMOOTH
MOVEMENT   *The back tuck (closed) position becomes unstable as the head is moved forward. The flexed head position shifts the center of gravity toward the feet. An upper-back shoulder press will result in the body rolling backward until the arms recover and catch at the mid-sculling depth. One of two different arm patterns may be used: 1. The recovery path of the arms may be initiated by rotating the upper arms and forearms outward while flexing*

*the elbows. The hands will pass inside the elbows close to the torso to catch near the mid body line and scull in front of the mid line of the body with the arms in the inverted **T** position. This arm pattern enables the swimmer to keep the upper arms nearly vertical and close to the ribs at the lateral body line (a position of good mechanical advantage for the tuck axial position). 2. The recovery path of the arms may be initiated by a slight inward rotation of the arms as they slip upward and outward toward the shoulders. When the hands are nearly shoulder-high, the arms are rotated outward, the forearms are flexed, and the* catch *is made prior to the inward sweep of the support sculling pattern at mid depth.*

Plate 31

a   b   c

Back Tuck (closed)   to   Back Tuck (closed)

Back Tuck Somersault Transition

BASIC
ELEMENTS   Support sculling, body press, support sculling

STABLE
POSITION   This position is held on the back at the water surface, as described in the kip tip up transition. Sculling is at the top depth.

SMOOTH
MOVEMENT   *The body is set in motion as described in the back tuck closed to the kip
tip up transition description. The body will continue to roll backward as the
arms recover to mid depth, followed by an outward press to the lateral line
of the body. The body will roll until the head is above the hips. At this
point sculling is resumed at top depth as the shoulders press toward the
back and the legs are raised to the water surface.* Refer to plate 31a for
the starting and finishing positions.

PLATE 32

a

b

c

Back Layout   to   Back Layout

Back Pike Somersault Transition

BASIC
ELEMENTS   Primary propulsion, body press, support sculling

STABLE
POSITION   The back layout starting position was described in the ballet leg transition no. 1.

SMOOTH
MOVEMENT   *To move from the back layout to the back pike position, movements occur nearly simultaneously. The arms rotate outward and vigorously scoop laterally from the hips to above the head. The lower abdominals contract, and the legs are flexed sharply at the hips. As the elbows reach shoulder level, the forearms are rotated inward, where sculling with the palms facing the water surface aids the descent of the upper torso. At the completion of the aerial leg pattern, the arms press to a vertical position, hands moving near the water surface.* (The total arm action is called circumflexion.) *As the legs pass through the vertical arms and begin to descend, the arms rotate inward at the shoulders and recover to sculling at the hips. A second scoop of less force and magnitude may be needed to propel the body. As the feet pass the bottom of the pattern the arms press forward; sculling is resumed at the hips to complete the transition. The legs are extended horizontally and the torso is pressed to a back layout position. The legs are adducted throughout the entire maneuver.* Refer to Plate 26a for the back layout starting and finishing positions.

PLATE 33

a

b

c   d

Back Layout   to   Ballet Legs Submarine, Double

Barracuda Transition

BASIC
ELEMENTS   Primary propulsion, body press, support sculling

STABLE
POSITION   The back layout position was described in ballet leg transition no. 1.

SMOOTH
MOVEMENT   *To move from the back layout to the submarine double ballet legs, three movements occur nearly simultaneously. The arms rotate outward and scoop laterally from the hips to near the shoulder level, then quickly recover to sculling at the hips. The lower abdominals contract, and the legs are flexed at the hips until at a ninety-degree angle to the water surface.* Refer to plate 26a for the beginning back layout position.

PLATE 34

a

b   c

Ballet Legs Submarine, Double   to   Ballet Leg Submarine, Single Variant

Heron Transition

BASIC
ELEMENTS   Support sculling, leg action

STABLE
POSITION   Sculling is at the hips. The legs are flexed at the hips and held at a ninety-
                  degree angle to the water surface. The torso is submerged on its back in a
                  horizontal position. The waterline is near the ankles. The legs are held
                  parallel by the adductors of the legs.

SMOOTH
MOVEMENT   *To move from the submarine double ballet legs to the submarine single
                  ballet leg variant, the hip flexors of one leg contract to move the thigh of
                  that leg toward the chest. The knee of that leg is flexed until the lower leg
                  is parallel to the water surface. The adductors of the legs hold the thighs
                  close together.* Refer to plate 34b for the submarine double ballet legs
                  starting position.

PLATE 35

a   b

Ballet Leg, Single   to   Ballet Leg, Single Variant

Flamingo Transition no. 1

BASIC
ELEMENTS   Support sculling, leg action

STABLE
POSITION   The body is on its back at the water surface in a nearly horizontal position.
One leg is airborne and held vertical to the water surface by the hip flexors
of that leg and the knee extensors. The opposite leg is held nearly horizontal
to the water surface by the hip extensors. To keep the ballet leg from
tilting to the left or right, the adductors and abductors counterbalance each
other. The lower abdominals contract to stabilize the pelvis. The head and
chest are horizontal at the water surface, with sculling at the top depth
rapid enough to support the airborne weight. Note: When the ballet leg
variant is to immediately follow the single ballet leg, the hips are allowed
to settle in the water so that during the movement of the horizontal thigh
the water line will not change.

SMOOTH
MOVEMENT   *To move from the single ballet leg to the single ballet leg variant, the thigh
of the horizontal leg is drawn toward the chest by the contraction of the
hip flexors of that leg; the foot and knee of the horizontal leg remain at
the water surface by limited action of the same muscles. The thigh moves
toward the chest until the lower leg is at mid calf to the vertical leg. The
adductors of the legs keep the thighs close together. Sculling is at top depth.*

PLATE 36

a

b

Ballet Leg, Single Variant   to   Ballet Legs, Double

Flamingo Transition

BASIC
ELEMENTS   Support sculling, airborne leg action

STABLE
POSITION   The torso is on its back at the water surface with one airborne leg vertical
to the water, the other leg flexed at the hip and knee until the lower leg
is at mid calf to the vertical leg. This position is stabilized by the holding
of the hip flexors, the lower abdominals, and the adductors of the legs. The
shoulders are slightly retracted. Sculling is deepened at the top depth in
preparation for the increased airborne weight.

SMOOTH
MOVEMENT   *To move from the single ballet leg variant to the double ballet legs, noticeable muscle action occurs at the knee joint. The knee extensors contract to
elevate the foot of the flexed leg. The hip flexors of that leg lengthen slightly
as the hip extensors pull the thigh to the vertical. The hip flexors and the
extensors then counterbalance to hold the legs vertical. The abdominals
hold the pelvis stable, and rapid sculling at or below the hips supports the
airborne weight. The legs are pressed parallel by the adductors of the legs.*
Refer to plate 36b for the single ballet leg variant starting position.

PLATE 37

a

b

Ballet Leg, Single   to   Ballet Leg Submarine, Single

Submarine Transition

BASIC
ELEMENTS   Static position and gravity

STABLE
POSITION   The static position of the single ballet leg was described in flamingo transition no. 1.

SMOOTH
MOVEMENT   *To move from the single ballet leg to the submarine single ballet leg, the head, shoulders, and the horizontal leg are pressed downward as the top depth sculling is released. Gravity will assist the descent. The pelvic area remains stable. The arms are rotated outward, followed by a scoop to the shoulder level. The forearms are flexed at the elbows and rotated inward until the palms face the water surface. A lateral recovery of the arms must draw the upper arms into the rib cage before the forearms slip to the hip area. The arms control both the forces of gravity and buoyancy once the descent has ceased by repeating small scoops of less force, followed by a recovery and momentary sculling at the hips.*

PLATE 38

a

b

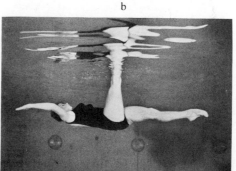

c   d

Ballet Legs, Double   to   Ballet Legs Submarine, Double

Submarine Double Ballet Legs Transition no. 1

BASIC
ELEMENTS   Static position and gravity

STABLE
POSITION   The torso is on its back at the water surface. Both legs are flexed at the
hips until perpendicular to the water surface. The torso is slightly flexed,
allowing the hips to stabilize at a deeper level than the chest and head.
Strong sculling at top depth below the hips will assist the swimmer in
holding this slightly flexed position. The chest is elevated by a slight
cervical arch. The head is held parallel to the water surface by the neck
extensors. The legs are pressed together by the adductors. The pelvis is
stabilized by a counterbalance of the lower abdominals and the hip extensors.

SMOOTH
MOVEMENT   *To descend, the torso and leg positions are held as sculling is released,
allowing gravity to pull the position downward in the water. Sculling at
the hips will terminate the descent as the water line is established no lower
than the ankles.*

PLATE 39

a

b

c

Ballet Leg Submarine, Single   to   Ballet Leg, Single

Submarine Ascent Transition

BASIC
ELEMENT   Propulsion sculling of a static position

STABLE
POSITION   The submarine single ballet leg position is basically the single ballet leg
                 position as described in flamingo transition no. 1 with the single exception
                 that it is submerged in the water to near ankle depth with the torso at
                 ninety degrees to the vertical leg. To control buoyancy at this level, the
                 swimmer must use small scoops followed by support sculling at the hips
                 and repeated as necessary.

SMOOTH
MOVEMENT   *To move from the submerged position to the water surface, the sculling
                 speed is increased. Sculling begins at a height near the knees. The body
                 will elevate upward through the arms. The pelvis and legs are held steady
                 during the ascent. The head and chest press to the surface as the hip
                 extensors contract to provide a high water line on the vertical leg.* Refer
                 to Plate 38d for the submarine single ballet leg starting position.

PLATE 40

a

b

c

Ballet Legs Submarine, Double   to   Ballet Legs, Double

Submarine Double Ballet Legs Ascent Transition

BASIC
ELEMENT   Propulsion sculling of a static position

STABLE
POSITION   The body is submerged no lower than the ankles. The torso and head are
horizontal; the legs are flexed at the hips until perpendicular to the water
surface. The hip flexors and extensors counterbalance to stablize the legs.
The pelvis is stabilized by the pull of the lower abdominals counterbalanced
by the hip extensors. The legs are adducted. Sculling is at hip level.

SMOOTH
MOVEMENT   *To move from the submarine double ballet legs to the double ballet legs
position at the water surface, sculling begins at mid thigh level. It must be
strong enough to elevate the body position as well as support the increasing
weight of the airborne legs. As the upward movement of the hips ceases,
the chest and head press to the water surface by means of a cervical arch.*
Refer to plate 39c for the submarine double ballet legs starting position.

PLATE 41

a

b

Ballet Leg Submarine, Single   to   Ballet Leg Submarine, Single

Single Ballet Leg Roll Transition

BASIC
ELEMENTS   Support sculling, body press, support sculling

STABLE
POSITION   The submarine single ballet leg position is stabilized by the same muscles
                  as described in the single ballet leg flamingo transition no. 1, with the
                  exceptions listed in the submarine ascent transition.

SMOOTH
MOVEMENT   *The starting and finishing positions are the same for this transition. The
                  body and one leg are nearly horizontal. A vertical leg is submerged to no
                  further than the ankle. The body begins a 360-degree roll around its
                  longitudinal axis in a direction opposite the ballet leg. The adductors of
                  the ballet leg pull that leg in the same direction of the body roll. As the
                  body approaches a roll of 180 degrees, it is unstable with buoyancy,
                  forcing it toward the surface. To overcome this force, the shoulders must
                  be pressed toward the back, causing the spine to extend. The arms aid the
                  body by making short pulls, and as the body moves onto its side, the arms
                  change to small scoops. The adductors of the ballet leg pull continuously
                  to provide motion around the longitudinal axis. The original starting posi-
                  tion is resumed.* Refer to plate 38c for the submarine single ballet leg
                  starting and finishing positions.

PLATE 42

a

b

c

d

e

f

Ballet Legs Submarine, Double   to   Ballet Legs Submarine, Double

Submarine Double Ballet Legs Roll Transition

BASIC
ELEMENTS   Support sculling, body press, support sculling

STABLE
POSITION   The submarine double ballet legs position is held as described in the sub-marine double ballet legs ascent transition.

SMOOTH
MOVEMENT   *The same muscular movement is used as described in the submarine single ballet leg roll transition except that as the legs move from a position of pointing toward the pool floor to pointing toward the water surface, the adductors and abductors of the legs assist in lifting the legs to vertical, where the water line is re-established no further than the ankles.* Refer to plate 39b for the submarine double ballet legs starting and finishing positions.

PLATE 43

a

b

c

d

e

Ballet Legs Submarine, Double   to   Ballet Leg Submarine, Single

Somersub and Subalina Transition

BASIC
ELEMENTS   Support sculling and leg action

STABLE
POSITION   The submarine double ballet legs position is held as described in the
                  submarine double ballet legs ascent transition.

SMOOTH
MOVEMENT   *From the submarine double ballet legs position, movement of one vertical
                  leg to the horizontal position is executed by first lengthening the hip flexors
                  of that leg. A slow release of these flexors and a steady pull of the same
                  leg extensors will move the leg until it is horizontal to the water surface.
                  The shoulders and head press downward slightly to offset the force of*

buoyancy and to establish a horizontal line. The hands aid the torso position by sculling with the palms facing the water surface. The pelvis is stabilized by a counterbalance of the lower abdominals and the hip extensors. The vertical leg is held motionless by a counterbalance of the hip flexors and extensors of that leg.

PLATE 44

a

b

c

Ballet Leg Submarine, Single   to   Vertical, Forward Split

Subcrane Transition

BASIC
ELEMENTS   Support sculling, body press, propulsion, support sculling

STABLE
POSITION   The submarine single ballet leg position was described in the submarine
                ascent transition.

SMOOTH
MOVEMENT   *To move from the submarine single ballet leg to the forward split vertical,
                the action is the same as used in the submarine single ballet leg roll until
                the body is prone, with the ballet leg pointing toward the pool floor. To
                move into the forward split vertical, the hip extensors must increase in
                pull and at the same time the chest is pressed downward. The arms pro-
                vide the propulsion by making a short pull, followed by a long scoop to raise
                the legs to the water surface. A rapid recovery from the scoop must move
                the arms to mid depth sculling, where the mechanical advantage is great
                enough to force the torso toward the surface feet-first.*

PLATE 45

a

b

c

d

e

f

Ballet Leg, Single.   to   Vertical, Front Pike

Eiffel Tower Transition

BASIC
ELEMENTS   Support sculling, body press, propulsion, support sculling

STABLE
POSITION   The single ballet leg was described in flamingo transition no. 1.

SMOOTH
MOVEMENT   *The single ballet leg is moved across the body by simple adduction of that
leg and controlled in its descent by the abductors. The lower torso rolls to
its side as the ballet leg approaches the water surface. The upper torso
rolls to the stomach and is then pressed downward and toward the feet.
The head is held in line with the torso on the descent. During the torso
descent, the adductors of the ballet leg pull to move that leg to the mid line of
the body. Strong hip extensors keep both legs at the surface. For aesthetic
purposes, the timing of the movement is important. The legs come in
contact with each other as the torso arrives at vertical. The torso pivot roll
action is enhanced by the arms. They are extended below the shoulders,
where the palms anchor against the water. A short scoop is followed by
a lateral pull toward the water surface. A rapid inward rotation of the arms
and flexion of the elbows will position the arms at mid-sculling depth
in time to support the front pike vertical stable position.*

PLATE 46

a

b

c

d

e

Ballet Leg, Single   to   Vertical, Forward Split

Crane Transition

BASIC
ELEMENTS   Support sculling, body press, support sculling

STABLE
POSITION   The single ballet leg was described in flamingo transition no. 1.

SMOOTH
MOVEMENT   *To move the torso from nearly horizontal to vertical, strong support sculling is essential near the hips at the top depth. The head aids the descent of the torso as it is slightly flexed during the downward press of the shoulders. During the torso descent, the hip extensors of the ballet leg hold that leg at a right angle to the horizontal leg. The hip flexors of the horizontal leg are in a strong, static contraction until that leg has been moved to the vertical. Both legs must travel an airborne arc of 90 degrees. As the ballet leg moves to the water, the hip flexors press that leg under the water to establish a horizontal line. By means of a recovery described in the kip tip up transition, the arms move from sculling at the top depth near the hips*

to support sculling at mid depth under the horizontal leg. The head is pressed in line with the torso as the legs are stabilized in the forward split vertical position.

PLATE 47

a

b

c

d

Ballet Leg, Single   to   Vertical, Forward Split

Catalina Transition, Conventional Method

BASIC
ELEMENTS   Support sculling, body press, support sculling

STABLE
POSITION   This transition is being performed in two distinctly different movements. For clarification, both the conventional and alternate methods are described. The single ballet leg was described in flamingo transition no. 1.

SMOOTH
MOVEMENT   *From support sculling at top depth, movement begins with a downward press of the shoulder opposite the ballet leg. During this press, the head is carried slightly flexed. The upper torso is rotated in a direction opposite to the ballet leg. During this action, the arm adjacent to the ballet leg is slipped across the lower torso to mid depth for support sculling. The chest is pressed forward as the head is extended to vertical alignment. (The torso action is referred to as a pivot-roll, a subtle movement in which the torso moves from horizontal to vertical by means of a shoulder press and spinal rotation.) There is a moment when both the horizontal and vertical legs pass through a point of increased extension. To do this, the flexors of the ballet leg must lengthen; the position of the legs is held by equalized static contraction of the abductors and adductors. If this were not true, the ballet leg would have a tendency to tilt in the direction of the torso rotation. Refer to plate 27b for the starting position.*

PLATE 48

a   b

Catalina Transition, Alternate Method

SMOOTH
MOVEMENT   *To move from the single ballet leg to the forward split vertical, the upper torso is pressed sideways through lateral flexion of the spine. The torso actually slips along the water surface to the side opposite the ballet leg. The down press of the shoulder opposite the ballet leg is joined by a slight flexion of the head. The upper torso rotates as the arms assume mid depth support sculling. To complete the movement, the lower torso is rotated and the shoulders press toward the back to establish the vertical. The head is moved to vertical alignment. The holding action of the horizontal leg is responsible for maintaining the relative position of that leg.* Refer to plate 27b for the single ballet leg starting position.

PLATE 49

a

b

c

d

e

f

Vertical, Forward Split   to   Ballet Leg, Single

Reverse Catalina Transition

BASIC
ELEMENTS   Support sculling, body press, support sculling

STABLE
POSITION   The torso and one leg are vertical. The pelvis is stabilized by a counterbal-
                ance of the lower back extensors and the lower abdominals. The second
                leg is held flexed at the hip in a nearly horizontal position at the water
                surface. The head and shoulders are in line with the hips, and the arms
                support the position by sculling at mid depth, employing the full range
                of movement within this depth.

SMOOTH
MOVEMENT   *To execute the reverse catalina transition, the shoulder adjacent to the
                vertical leg is pressed toward the back. The opposite shoulder is pressed
                forward. During this torso movement, the upper arms remain near the
                lateral body line, and in that position they move with the torso. As the
                pelvis rotates toward the ballet leg, the forearm adjacent to that leg slips
                across the lower abdomen to support scull at the hips as the chest and head
                are pressed upward to a horizontal position. The pelvis and legs are stabil-*

ized during the torso action by the hip flexors and the extensors along with the lower abdominals. The head travels in line with the shoulders throughout the transition.

PLATE 50

a

b

c

Ballet Leg Submarine, Single   to   Vertical, Forward Split

Subalina Transition

BASIC
ELEMENTS   Support sculling, body press, support sculling

STABLE
POSITION   The submarine single ballet leg is stablized by the same muscles as described
                  in the single ballet leg flamingo transition no. 1, with the exception listed
                  in the submarine ascent transition.

SMOOTH
MOVEMENT   *To move from the submarine single ballet leg position to the forward split*

vertical, the movement is the same as described in the catalina transition, with the following additions: as the upper torso is pressed downward, the result of this press thrusts the hips toward the surface; sculling begins at mid-thigh depth, the upper arms move with the rotation of the upper torso and remain along the lateral body line; support sculling is resumed at the mid depth during the vertical alignment of the upper torso.

PLATE 51

a

b

c

Back Layout   to   Vertical, Front Pike

Albatross Transition

BASIC
ELEMENTS   Primary propulsion, body press, support sculling

STABLE
POSITION   The back layout position was described in ballet leg transition no. 1. In addition to that description, the arms are extended beyond the head at the surface of the water.

SMOOTH
MOVEMENT   *Movement begins by sculling in a headfirst direction. The head and shoulders moving as one unit, gradually press downward as the rate of propulsion is increased. During the torso descent, the hip extensors, counterbalanced by contraction of the lower abdominals, hold the legs and hips at the water surface. When the head and shoulders approach the quarter point of an imaginary circle, one shoulder is pressed downward. The torso and legs then rotate toward that shoulder. The chest and head press toward the front of the body as the arms pull toward the water surface. As the upper arms move alongside the lateral line of the torso, they rotate inward, allowing the forearms to catch and scull at the mid depth. The front pike vertical is stabilized by a counterbalance of the hip flexors and extensors, aided by static holding of the lower abdominals.*

PLATE 52

a

b

c

Vertical   to   Vertical, Forward Split

Dolpholina Transition

BASIC
ELEMENTS   Propulsion, leg action, support sculling

STABLE
POSITION   In the dolpholina transition, a vertical is executed. It is the result of body
alignment during propulsion of a foot-first circle. The muscles and liga-
ments of the body are responsible for this position. A vertical position
is perpendicular to the water surface with the head downward. The
weight-bearing parts are in balance with each other so as to decrease the
muscular force necessary to maintain the position. The center of gravity of
the body is moved toward the front of the body and toward the head.
The upper arms are slightly to the front of the body and held nearly level
with the shoulders. The forearms are positioned vertically, flexed at the
elbows, and rotated inward so that the hyperextended hands hold the fingers
so that they point toward the back of the swimmer, with the palms facing
the pool floor. The vertical line is an imaginary line that runs through
certain anatomical markings of the body when it is headfirst in the water.
Those markings are the outside of the little toe, the outer ankle bone, the
outside center of the knee joint, the outside center of the pelvis, the
outside center of the shoulder, and the ear lobe (see drawing of vertical
on page p. 38).

SMOOTH
MOVEMENT   *To move into the forward split vertical, the vertical body ascends feet-first
as a result of buoyancy and mid sculling forces. As the toes become airborne, one leg is lowered to the water surface by a gradual release of the
hip extensors of that leg. The pelvis is stabilized by the counterbalance of*

PLATE 53

a

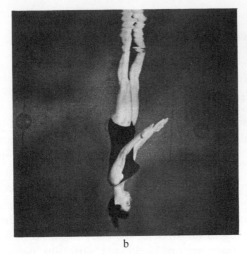

b   c

the lower abdominals and the lower back extensors. Sculling at mid depth supports the airborne weight. The vertical leg is held by static contraction of the adductors and abductors.

Vertical, Forward Split   to   Vertical, Forward Split

180-Degree Twist Transition

BASIC
ELEMENTS   Support sculling, body press, and a minimum of propulsion by the arms

STABLE
POSITION   The forward split vertical was described in the reverse catalina transition.

SMOOTH
MOVEMENT   *Sculling is at mid depth, supporting the airborne weight and assisting to twist clockwise around the longitudinal axis of the body when the right leg is horizontal. Movement begins by adducting the horizontal leg. The torso is rotated by pressing the right shoulder forward as the hands press outward from the mid-body line. The left shoulder is pressed toward the back as the forearms press inward toward the mid-body line. The relationship of rotation between the torso and horizontal leg is critical in this transition because, if the trunk rotates more rapidly than the horizontal leg, balance is lost. Holding the position of the vertical leg is also a critical balance factor. This leg is forcefully stretched upward, with additional emphasis on the abductors of that leg. When the left leg is horizontal, the rotational direction reverses.*

PLATE 54

a

b

c

Vertical, Low Water Line   to   Vertical, Low Water Line

Twisting at Ankle or Mid Calf Transition

BASIC
ELEMENTS   A combination of support and propulsion sculling with body press

STABLE
POSITION   The body is fully extended and in vertical balance as described in the dolpholina transition, with the exception that the water line is constant, with the arms in the inverted, modified **L** position, bottom depth (see figure 16 on page 38).

SMOOTH
MOVEMENT   *Movement in a clockwise direction around the longitudinal axis of the body is performed by support sculling and a slight rotational press of the body. The right side of the torso is pressed forward as the hands scull outward from the mid-body line at bottom depth. The right hand assists this press. As the arms scull inward toward the mid line, the left side of the torso is pressed toward the back. The left hand assists this movement. Because the body is in line and nearly submerged, a very slight pressure against the water will set it in motion. The vertical line is distinguished by the same anatomical markings as listed in the dolpholina transition; the legs are firmly adducted and stretched. A twist may be 180 or 360 degrees.*

PLATE 55

a

b

c

Vertical   to   Vertical

High Water Line Twist, Crane, and Contra-Crane Transition

BASIC
ELEMENT   Support sculling with limited body press

STABLE
POSITION   The vertical alignment of the body was described in the dolpholina transi-
                 tion. However, to support a high water line, the position of the arms is
                 described as the inverted **T** and sculling is at mid depth (see figure 17 on
                 page 38). The coordinated action of the arms with the body rotation was
                 described in the transition, vertical low water line twist. However, to
                 support a high water line the arms must scull at mid depth to maintain
                 height.

SMOOTH
MOVEMENT   *Movies and loop films do not reveal the hidden muscular action of the
                 high water line twist. Therefore, help the swimmer coordinate the subtle
                 muscle action by suggesting she think of gradually pressing the right shoulder
                 forward as the arms sweep outward from the mid line of the body, and
                 pressing the left shoulder backward as the arms sweep inward. This will
                 create a clockwise twist.*

PLATE 56

Vertical, Low Water Line   to   Ballet Legs Submarine, Double

Elevator Transition

BASIC
ELEMENTS   Support sculling, body press, support sculling

STABLE
POSITION   The vertical, low water line was described in the dolpholina transition.

SMOOTH
MOVEMENT   *This transition begins in a vertical position, with the arms sculling at the bottom depth, in the inverted, modified L position (see figure 16 on page 38). During the torso movement from vertical to horizontal, the arm pattern is unique: downward pressure against the water is executed as the hands move from a deep position to a shallow one in front of the face; the upper arms move inward (adduction) toward the lateral line of the upper torso; the forearms rotate outward and are sharply flexed. This moves the arms into the inverted T position. The abdominals contract to press the torso from vertical to horizontal. This is not a curling action of the trunk; the torso moves around the vertical legs; the head is carried in line with the shoulders. Immediately following the abdominal contraction, the forearms are rotated inward and extended to support sculling at the hips, top depth. The legs remain relatively stationary by the holding action of the hip extensors.*

PLATE 57

a   b

c   d

Axial, Tuck Tip Up   to   Vertical, High Water Line

Kip Transition

**BASIC
ELEMENTS**   Support sculling, body press, airborne leg action, support sculling

**STABLE
POSITION**   The tuck axial is a position in which the legs are flexed and adducted.
The abdominals are contracted to flatten the natural arch of the lower
back, the pelvis is tipped backward, moving the lower abdominal area
toward the stomach. The upper torso and head are flexed, and the shoulders
are protracted. The arms scull at mid depth in the inverted **T** position. The
body is balanced and static, floating on its shoulders upside down at the
water surface with the feet and lower legs perpendicular to the surface.

**SMOOTH
MOVEMENT**   *Movement begins as the hip extensors straighten the legs to vertical. This
is a very difficult movement to learn because the lower legs must remain
vertical during the elevation of the thighs. At first only the thighs appear
to pivot around the knees, however, once the thighs are horizontal, the knees
appear to pivot around the hips. The swimmer must learn to lift the feet and
press the back of the knees toward a line perpendicular to the water surface.
Just prior to the vertical alignment of the legs, the upper torso and head
press to vertical. A counterbalance of the lower abdominals with the lower-
back extensors stabilize the pelvis during the shifting weight of the legs*

and at vertical alignment of the total body. The arms scull throughout the range of the mid depth and arrive at the lateral body line as the vertical is established. Because the timing of this transitional movement is extremely relevant to the establishment of vertical, and because its complexity involves maximum height of the airborne legs accompanied by a torso press, the kip figure is too advanced for novice synchronized swimmers.

PLATE 58

a

b

c

d

Ballet Leg Submarine, Single Variant   to   Vertical, Variant

Heron Transition

BASIC
ELEMENTS   Support sculling, body press, support sculling

STABLE
POSITION   The torso is horizontal. One leg is flexed at the hip until perpendicular to the water surface; the opposite leg is flexed at both the hip and knee. From knee to foot, this leg is held parallel to the water surface by the flexors of the knee. This position is held submerged in the water, with the water line near the ankles, no lower than the ankles. Support sculling is at the hips.

SMOOTH
MOVEMENT   *Movement is begun by placing the hands in a sculling position approximately at the depth of the bent knee. The head is in line with the shoulders. As one unit, the head and shoulders press downward. The abdominals are not allowed to stretch during the early stages of the shoulder press, which results in elevation of the hips and legs. There is no exaggerated backward tilt of the pelvis causing a thrust, but rather a slow rise of the lower back. As the torso moves downward, the thigh of the bent leg is moved toward the chest. At the point of vertical, the downward press is counterbalanced by the lower abdominals. The adductors of both legs hold the thighs close together. Just prior to vertical, the forearms slip inward toward the body and catch the water at the mid-sculling depth.*

PLATE 59

a

b   c

Ballet Legs, Double   to   Vertical, High Water Line

Flamingo Transition

BASIC
ELEMENTS   Support sculling, body press, support sculling

STABLE
POSITION   The double ballet legs position was described in the submarine double
                      ballet legs transition no. 1.

SMOOTH
MOVEMENT   *To move from the double ballet legs to the vertical high water line, strong
                      support sculling below the hips at top depth is executed. The shoulders,
                      with the head slightly flexed, are pressed downward. As the upper torso
                      begins to descend, the abdominals are not allowed to stretch, resulting in
                      elevation of the hips. This is not a hip thrust in which the abdominals
                      rapidly pull to change the pelvic position. The pelvis is stabilized near the
                      water surface by the counterbalance of the abdominals and hip extensors.
                      The hip flexors slightly release as the vertical is established. Just prior to
                      vertical, the forearms slip toward the body and the hands catch at mid
                      depth, near the lateral body line. Maximum height is the result of making
                      the catch along the lateral line of the body in the inverted* **T** *position,
                      followed by a feather press downward.* Refer to plate 39a for the double
                      ballet legs starting position.

PLATE 60

a

b

c

d

Ballet Legs Submarine, Double   to   Vertical, High Water Line

Barracuda Transition

BASIC
ELEMENTS   Support sculling, body press, support sculling

STABLE
POSITION   The submarine double ballet legs position was described in the submarine
double ballet legs roll transition.

SMOOTH
MOVEMENT   *Movement begins when the arms reach to knee depth and scull to elevate
the position. When the water line is at the knees, the shoulders press downward and the head is flexed. The lower abdominals pull to thrust the hips,
and the legs stretch upward. As the shoulders and head complete their
press to vertical, the forearms slip inward toward the body, enabling the
hands to catch at mid depth. Following the catch, a press to the lateral
body line positions the arms for the feather press* (lateral scoop) *enabling
the swimmer to achieve maximum height. The pelvis is stabilized to maintain vertical by a counterbalance of the hip extensors and lower abdominals.
The legs are adducted throughout the transition.*

PLATE 61

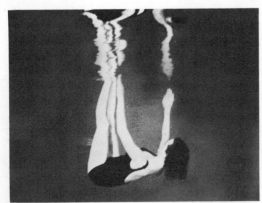

a

b

c

Ballet Leg, Single   to   Axial, Reverse Split

Knight Transition

BASIC
ELEMENTS   Support sculling, body press, support sculling

STABLE
POSITION   The single ballet leg was described in flamingo transition no. 1.

SMOOTH
MOVEMENT   *Top depth sculling is used during the torso descent. Movement from the single ballet leg to the reverse split axial is executed by bringing the head into a slightly flexed position as the shoulders press downward through an arc. The pelvis remains stationary during the torso descent, resulting in an arch in the lower back. During the movement through the arc, the flexors holding the ballet leg increase in length. Adduction of the legs hold the thighs close together. As the upper torso passes under the hips, the upper abdominal muscles pull to aid the vertical alignment. The shoulders are straightened, and the head is moved in line. The arms recover to the mid depth and press to the lateral line for support of the reverse split axial.*

PLATE 62

a   b

c

d

Axial, Reverse Split   to   Vertical, Forward Split

Castle Transition

BASIC
ELEMENTS   Support sculling, airborne leg action, support sculling

STABLE
POSITION   The reverse split axial is stabilized by sculling at the mid depth along the
                lateral line of the body. The torso is vertical, with the head in line. The
                lower back is arched, allowing the pelvis to tip forward. The hip flexors
                of the vertical leg hold that leg airborne, whereas the hip extensors hold
                the horizontal leg at the water surface.

SMOOTH
MOVEMENT   *Movement begins with the hip flexors of the horizontal leg. Contraction of
                these muscles lifts the horizontal leg to vertical. The leg continues its
                aerial pattern and is lowered to the water surface by a slow lengthening
                of the hip extensors controlling that leg. The pelvic arch is removed by
                lower abdominal contraction. The vertical ballet leg is controlled by a
                counterbalance of the hip flexors and the extensors of that leg. The arms
                support this transition by sculling at mid depth, making use of the full
                range within this depth.*

PLATE 63

a

b

c

Axial, Reverse Split   to   Vertical, Forward Split

Aurora Transition

BASIC
ELEMENTS   Support sculling, body press, support sculling

STABLE
POSITION   The reverse split axial was described in the castle transition.

SMOOTH
MOVEMENT   *Movement begins as the shoulder adjacent to the horizontal leg presses backward. Both legs rotate about their longitudinal axis and remain in the same relative plane to the body as the torso completes a twist of 180 degrees. During this pivoting, twisting action, the horizontal leg passes through adduction, followed by slight flexion at the hip joint. The vertical*

leg is abducted, followed by adduction. The arms remain in the inverted **T** *position while sculling throughout the range of the mid depth.*

PLATE 64

a

b

c

Vertical, Forward Split   to   Axial, Reverse Split

Aurora Open 180 Degrees Transition

BASIC ELEMENTS	Support sculling, airborne leg action, support sculling
STABLE POSITION	The forward split vertical was described in the reverse catalina transition. Pictures show a portion of the path taken by one leg. Sequence is incomplete.
SMOOTH MOVEMENT	*Moving as one complete lever, the horizontal leg is abducted forcefully enough to swing it 360 degrees. The momentum gained from this leg aids*

the torso in twisting 180 degrees around its longitudinal axis, moving in the same direction as the horizontal leg. The arms remain in the inverted **T** *position, sculling at mid depth, using the full range of this depth.*

PLATE 65

a

b

c

d

Vertical, Forward Split   to   Axial, Split

Subalarc Transition

BASIC
ELEMENTS   Support sculling, airborne leg action, support sculling

STABLE
POSITION   The forward split vertical has been described in the reverse catalina transition.

SMOOTH
MOVEMENT   *While sculling at mid depth with the arms in the inverted* **T** *position, movement begins by raising the horizontal leg to vertical by means of contracting the hip extensors. At the vertical, both legs begin to move. The horizontal leg, now vertical, is lowered toward the back of the swimmer until it rests at the water surface. This movement is performed by the lengthening of the hip flexors. The vertical leg is lowered to the water in front of the swimmer by a slow lengthening of the hip extensors controlling that leg. The lower back arches (pelvic tilt forward) to aid the degree of split axial position. The hips are not allowed to rotate around the spine to any noticeable degree; nor are the legs permitted to rotate around their longitudinal axis. Each leg is held in line with the hip by static contraction of the adductors and abductors. The upper torso and head remain in line throughout this transition.*

PLATE 66

a

b

c

Back Layout   to   Axial, Split

Walkover Back Transition

BASIC
ELEMENTS   Propulsion sculling, body press, airborne leg action, support sculling

STABLE
POSITION   The back layout was described in ballet leg transition no. 1, with the exception that in preparation for this transition, the arms are extended above the head.

SMOOTH
MOVEMENT   *The arms propel the body headfirst from an overhead position. The head and shoulders press downward as the body descends. It is necessary to draw the hips under the surface before the horizontal leg begins its arc. The hip flexors of this leg contract to move it to vertical. It is lowered to the water surface in front of the swimmer by a gradual release of the hip extensors. The head and shoulders press toward the front of the body; the upper arms adduct and flex at the elbows. Only a pelvic arch remains. Support sculling in the lateral line at mid depth stabilizes this position.*

PLATE 67

a   b

c

d

Back Layout   to   Vertical

Spiral Transition

BASIC ELEMENTS	Propulsion sculling, body press, airborne leg action, support sculling
STABLE POSITION	The back layout was described in ballet leg transition no. 1, with the exception that for this transition the arms are overhead at the surface.
SMOOTH MOVEMENT	*This transition begins with sculling headfirst overhead. The head and shoulders press downward until the head has traversed more than one quarter of a circle. A maximum arch in the back is used momentarily. The abdominals and hip flexors contract to lift the legs to vertical. Just prior to the lift of the legs, the upper arms are adducted and the forearms flex, moving the arms to the mid sculling depth. Strong sculling at the lateral body line will assist the lift of the legs. As the vertical is established, to sustain height the arms scull near the lateral body line at mid depth in the inverted* **T** *position.*

PLATE 68

a

b

c

d

Back Layout   to   Vertical, High Water Line

Contra-Crane Transition

BASIC
ELEMENTS   Propulsion sculling, body press, propulsion, support sculling

STABLE
POSITION   The back layout was described in ballet leg transition no. 1, with the ex-
                 ception that the arms are above the head at the water surface.

SMOOTH
MOVEMENT   *Movement begins by sculling overhead in a headfirst direction. The*
                 shoulders and head press downward as one unit. As in a dolphin figure, the
                 descent continues until the feet are just under the water surface. The lower
                 abdominals pull to straighten the lower back as the upper abdominals aid
                 the chest press to vertical. Sculling is at the lateral line and mid depth.
                 Buoyancy and sculling elevate the body feet-first until a high water line
                 is established.

PLATE 69

a

b

c

d

e

Axial, Reverse Split	to	Vertical, Variant

Knight Transition

<table>
<tr><td>BASIC
ELEMENTS</td><td>Support sculling, airborne leg action, support sculling</td></tr>
<tr><td>STABLE
POSITION</td><td>The reverse split axial was described in the castle transition.</td></tr>
<tr><td>SMOOTH
MOVEMENT</td><td>Movement begins when the hip flexors of the horizontal leg contract to lift that leg to vertical. At the same time, a slow lengthening of the hip and knee extensors of the vertical leg allows gravity to flex the hip and knee</td></tr>
</table>

joints of that leg. The result moves the vertical foot along the vertical line. The lower abdominals pull to align the lower spine as the vertical leg stretches upward. The vertical variant position requires slight adduction of the flexed leg. Sculling is at mid depth, near the lateral line.

PLATE 70

a

b

c

Axial, Split   to   Back Layout

Walkover Front Transition no. 1

BASIC
ELEMENTS   Support sculling, airborne leg action, buoyancy uplift

STABLE
POSITION   The split axial position is stabilized by keeping the upper torso and head in a vertical line while the pelvis is tipped forward to enhance the splits.

Sculling is along the lateral line of the body at mid depth. One leg is held extended onto the back while the other is flexed at the hip.

SMOOTH
MOVEMENT

To move from the split axial to the back layout, the arms are placed near the water surface at the top of the mid sculling depth. The hands will be near the knees of the piked leg. As the piked leg is raised through the airborne arc to the vertical by contraction of the hip extensors, the arms press firmly downward and to the lateral line of the body. The area covered represents the range of the mid sculling depth; the movement provides maximum height. As the moving leg passes the vertical, the flexors stretch to control the lowering of that leg to the water surface. The back arches as the shoulders and head press toward the surface. The arms press to bottom depth sculling, where the position (arched axial) becomes unstable due to buoyancy forcing the body upward and toward the feet. The hip extensors press the hips to the surface, and the leg flexors keep the legs from sinking. The head and chest press upward gradually as the layout is assumed. The abductors of the legs hold the thighs parallel throughout the maneuver.

PLATE 71

a

b

c

d

Axial, Split   to   Front Layout

Walkover Back Transition

BASIC
ELEMENTS   Support sculling, airborne leg action, primary propulsion

STABLE
POSITION   The split axial was described in walkover front transition no. 1.

SMOOTH
MOVEMENT   *From the split axial position, movement involves hip flexion of the hori-
                zontal leg to the back of the body. These flexor muscles slowly raise that
                leg to vertical, moving it through an airborne arc. The hip extensors of
                that leg slowly release, allowing the leg to traverse the remainder of the
                arc and ease into its place at the surface of the water along side the piked
                leg. The hip extensors hold both legs at the surface during the torso ascent.
                Movement toward the feet is continued as buoyancy, aided by a scoop of
                the arms, elevates the torso to the water surface in a front layout position.*

PLATE 72

a

b

c

Front Layout   to   Front Layout, Variant

Swordfish Transition no. 1

BASIC
ELEMENTS   Support sculling, leg action

STABLE
POSITION   The body is at the water surface in a horizontal (prone) position. This
                position is maintained by a counterbalance of the hip extensors and the
                abdominal muscles. The head is held hyperextended with the chin at the
                water surface, or extended with the face in the water. The legs are held
                parallel by adduction and fully extended with the heels at the surface.
                Support sculling at the top depth near the hips aids the horizontal line.

SMOOTH
MOVEMENT   *Movement begins by flexing the thigh of one leg at the hip and knee joints until perpendicular to the water surface. The foot of the moving leg is pressed along the inside of the horizontal leg by constant adduction. Sculling is at top depth near the hips.*

PLATE 73

a

b

c

Front Layout   to   Front Tuck

Forward Tuck Somersault Transition

BASIC
ELEMENTS   Support sculling, leg action, body press

STABLE
POSITION   The front layout position has been described in the swordfish transition.

SMOOTH
MOVEMENT

Movement begins by drawing the thighs toward the chest. The thighs move under the hips and lower abdomen. The knees are flexed to maximum so that the lower legs are parallel to the water surface. The abdominals contract and the shoulders are protracted. The head flexes to complete the curved line of the spine. Sculling remains near the hips.

PLATE 74

a

b

Front Tuck   to   Front Layout

Front Tuck Somersault Transition

BASIC
ELEMENTS

Propulsion, body press, leg action. support sculling

STABLE
POSITION

The front tuck position requires holding the legs in a tightly flexed position. The abdominals are pulling, causing the back to become round in appearance. The shoulders are protracted and the face is in the water. Sculling is near the shoulder level at the top depth.

SMOOTH
MOVEMENT

The front tuck position becomes unstable when the head is lowered in the water. Beginning at a point below the shoulders, the arms pull to maximum

hyperextension, as shown below. The body passes through the arms, allowing a release of this position to a position from which the swimmer may scoop the forearms toward the head after outward rotation of the arms. The elevation of the upper arms to the level of the shoulders will assist the torso ascent. As the upper torso assumes a horizontal position at the water surface, the arms pull toward the feet. The tuck is straightened by the extensors of the body as the arms scoop from hip to shoulder level and resume support sculling at the top depth. Refer to plate 74b for the starting position.

PLATE 75

a

b

d

e

Front Layout   to   Vertical, Front Pike

Porpoise Transition

BASIC
ELEMENTS   Primary propulsion, body press, support sculling

STABLE
POSITION   The front layout position was described in the swordfish transition.

SMOOTH
MOVEMENT

To move from the front layout to the front pike vertical position, the face is placed in the water with the ears in line with the shoulders; the arms are lowered below the shoulders. From this point, the swimmer has a multiple choice of propulsion patterns.

1. *The forearms may be rotated outward as a small scoop is executed, and immediately rotated inward for a small pull. This pattern may be repeated, moving the upper arms toward the water surface as the chest presses downward.*

2. *The forearms may be extended below the waist, with the upper arms along the lateral line of the body and slightly to the front of the chest. By flexing and extending the arms (reverse dog paddle) the downward press of the chest is accomplished with great ease.*

3. *The arms may be extended below the shoulders and rotated inward in preparation for a large pull toward the feet then outward from the sides of the upper torso. During this arm action the upper abdominals press the chest downward.*

The lower abdominals and hip extensors hold the legs at the water surface, and the back remains relatively flat during the torso descent. The muscular movement used in piking needs to be identified on land for the swimmers. When in the water, the swimmer cannot keenly feel the action; nor is it readily possible to isolate the action of the upper and lower abdominals. Refer to plate 72a for the front layout starting position.

PLATE 76

a

b

c

d

Vertical, Front Pike   to   Axial, Split

Walkover Front Transition

BASIC
ELEMENTS   Support sculling, airborne leg action, support sculling

STABLE
POSITION   The front pike vertical is held by the hip flexors holding the legs at a
                  ninety-degree angle to the trunk. The legs are at the surface, whereas from
                  hip to head the body is vertical. The lower abdominals hold the pelvis
                  in line with the shoulders. The legs are adducted, fully extended, and the
                  toes are plantar-flexed. Sculling is at mid depth with the arms in the
                  inverted **T** position.

SMOOTH
MOVEMENT   *From the front pike vertical position, the hip extensors of one leg lift that
                  leg to vertical. The hip flexors of that same leg slowly release to control
                  the lowering of the leg to the water surface in back of the swimmer. The
                  piked leg remains at the water surface in front of the swimmer by a holding
                  of the flexors of that leg. The lower abdominals slowly release to allow the
                  pelvis to tilt. Sculling at the top of the mid depth aids the lift of the leg.
                  The arms move to the lateral line of the body as the moving leg passes ver-
                  tical. This arm action represents the use of the mid-depth range.*

PLATE 77

a

b

c

d

Vertical, Front Pike   to   Ballet Legs Submarine, Double

Beginning Transition for Many Figures

BASIC
ELEMENTS   Propulsion of a static position, support

STABLE
POSITION   The front pike vertical was described in the walkover front transition.

SMOOTH
MOVEMENT   *From a front pike vertical, the body is propelled head first around its lateral axis by a single pull or several short pulls of the arms originating beyond the head and traversing from in front of the body to the lateral line of the body. The arms rotate inward during the pull. As the body rotates around the arms, the pull is toward the hips. During the propulsion phase, the piked body position is held by the hip flexors. As the torso moves from vertical to horizontal, the abdominals lengthen and the hip extensors counterbalance the flexors to aid the establishment of vertical thighs. As the abdominals stretch, the extensors of the head align the head with the shoulders. Sculling at the hips may include an occasional half scoop to offset buoyancy.*

PLATE 78

a

b

c

d

Vertical, Front Pike   to   Front Layout

Front Pike Somersault Transition

BASIC
ELEMENTS   Propulsion of a static position, support sculling, leg action

STABLE
POSITION   The front pike vertical position was described in the walkover front transi-
                tion.

SMOOTH
MOVEMENT   *The front pike position is held by the hip flexors during propulsion of the
                front pike somersault. Movement begins when the arms are rotated inward
                and pressed toward the water surface and to the back of the body, fol-
                lowed by a downward pull toward the front of the body. The body moves
                headfirst around its lateral axis in the piked position, stablized at the hips
                by a counterbalance of the hip flexors and extensors. The torso will move
                around an imaginary square design. Sculling at the hips will support the
                trunk in its final front layout position as the hip extensors press the legs
                to the surface. The legs are adducted throughout the design.* Refer to plate
                76d for the starting position of the front pike vertical.

PLATE 79

a

b

c

d

e

f

g

Vertical, Front Pike   to   Vertical, Forward Split

Eiffel Tower Transition

BASIC
ELEMENTS   Support sculling, airborne leg action, support sculling

STABLE
POSITION   The front pike vertical was described in the walkover front transition.

SMOOTH
MOVEMENT   *Movement begins as one leg is raised to the vertical by the hip extensors*
                of that leg. The trunk and head remain in line throughout the transition.
                Support sculling is at mid depth with the arms in the inverted **T** *position.*

PLATE 80

a

b

c

Vertical, Front Pike   to   Vertical, Variant

Albatross Transition

BASIC
ELEMENTS   Support sculling, airborne leg action, support sculling

STABLE
POSITION   The front pike vertical position was described in the walkover front transition.

SMOOTH
MOVEMENT   *Movement begins as the hip extensors contract to lift one leg to the vertical. The hip flexors of the opposite leg flex the knee of that leg until the foot contacts inside the thigh of the vertical leg. The legs are adducted, keeping the thighs close together. The lower abdominals and hip extensors counterbalance to stabilize the pelvis. The trunk remains in line throughout. Support sculling is at mid depth, in the inverted **T** position.*

PLATE 81

a

b

c

Vertical, Forward Split   to   Axial, Split

Catalarc Open 180 Degrees Transition

BASIC
ELEMENTS   Support sculling, leg action, support sculling

STABLE
POSITION   The forward split vertical position was described in the reverse catalina transition.

SMOOTH
MOVEMENT   *Movement begins in the horizontal leg. It is raised to the vertical by the extensor muscles. Without hesitation or loss of height, the body is propelled through a one-half twist. Both legs are lowered to the water, resulting in a split axial. A gradual release of the hip flexors controls the movement of the leg to the back of the body; whereas a gradual release of the leg extensors controls the leg to the front of the body. The pelvis is tipped forward to enhance the split position. Sculling is at mid depth.*

Front Layout   to   Vertical, Forward Split

Hightower Transition

BASIC
ELEMENTS   Body press with primary propulsion, airborne leg action, support sculling

STABLE
POSITION   The front layout position was described in the swordfish transition.

SMOOTH
MOVEMENT   *Movement begins as the back is arched, followed by a strong scoop of the arms. The hip extensors pull one leg through an airborne arc. As this leg is raised, the chest is pressed downward in the water. The arms recover to the front of the body and scull at mid depth, supporting the airborne leg. The body arch is released as the lower abdominals pull to align the pelvis vertically. The upper abdominals aid the forward press of the chest to vertical. Throughout this transition, one leg is held at the water surface by the hip flexors of that leg.*

PLATE 82

a

b

c

Vertical, Forward Split   to   Ballet Leg, Single

Contra-Crane Transition

BASIC
ELEMENTS   Support sculling, slight body press, support sculling

STABLE
POSITION   The forward split vertical position was described in the reverse catalina transition.

SMOOTH
MOVEMENT   *From the forward split vertical position, movement is toward the back of the body. A gentle press of the hands toward the pool floor along the lateral body line accompanied by a slight release of the lower abdominals*

129

will rotate the body backwards around its lateral axis. Support sculling at the hips, buoyancy, and a chest press upward will elevate the body to the single ballet leg position. A picture of the single ballet leg is not shown in this sequence.

PLATE 83

a

b

c

d

Front Variant   to   Axial, Split Variant

Swordfish Transition no. 2

BASIC
ELEMENTS   Primary propulsion, body press, support sculling

STABLE
POSITION   The front layout position was described in swordfish transition no. 1. This
                  position becomes the front variant when one leg is flexed at the hip and
                  knee joints until the thigh of that leg is perpendicular to the water surface.
                  The foot of the flexed leg is pressed against the thigh of the extended leg.
                  Both legs are adducted. Sculling at top depth between the hips and shoulders
                  supports the front variant position.

SMOOTH
MOVEMENT   *Movement begins as the back is arched, followed by a strong scoop of
                  the arms. The hip extensors pull the horizontal leg through an airborne
                  arc of 180 degrees. As this leg is raised, the chest is pressed downward in
                  the water. The arms recover to mid-depth sculling near the lateral body
                  line, where another short scoop is executed. As the airborne leg passes
                  the mid arc, the head and shoulders press toward the water surface. The
                  arms scull at bottom depth under the extended leg to stabilize the split
                  axial variant position.*

PLATE 84

a

b

c

Front Variant   to   Ballet Leg Submarine, Single Variant

Swordalina Transition

BASIC
ELEMENTS   Primary propulsion, body press, support sculling

STABLE
POSITION   The front variant was described in swordfish transition no. 2.

SMOOTH
MOVEMENT   *As in the swordfish transition, movement begins as the back is arched, followed by a strong scoop of the arms. The hip extensors pull the horizontal leg through an airborne arc until the foot of that leg is above and in line with the head. Sculling is resumed at mid depth, with the upper arms pressed toward the back. The head and shoulders are moved forward, followed by a backward press of the shoulders adjacent to the ballet leg. The torso moves toward the ballet leg through a pivot roll. Strong adduction of the bent leg aids this movement. The upper arms remain close to the rib cage, where sculling supports the height of the body. As the torso completes the roll to the back, the forearms rotate inward and scull at the hips. The flexors of the bent leg are slightly released, causing the foot of that leg to move away from the vertical leg. The chest is pressed toward the water surface to establish the submarine single ballet leg variant position.*

132

PLATE 85

a

b

c

Front Variant   to   Ballet Leg, Single

Swordasub Transition

BASIC ELEMENTS   Primary propulsion, body press, support sculling, airborne leg action

STABLE POSITION   The body is prone at the water surface. The head is either extended so that the face is in the water or hyperextended so that the water line is at the chin. One leg is flexed at the hip and knee joints until the thigh of that leg is perpendicular to the water surface. The foot of the flexed leg is pressed against the thigh of the extended leg. Both legs are adducted. Support sculling is at top depth between the hips and shoulders. The water line touches outside the ankle bone of the horizontal leg and passes through a portion of the thigh, the hips, and the shoulders.

133

SMOOTH
MOVEMENT   *As in the swordfish and swordalina transitions, movement begins as the back is arched, followed by a strong scoop of the arms. The hip extensors pull the horizontal leg through an airborne arc of 180 degrees. As this leg traverses the arc, the chest is pressed downward in the water. The arms recover to support sculling at the hips. The flexed leg is extended at the knee to a ballet leg position. The head and chest press toward the water surface until the single ballet leg position is established at the surface of the water.*

PLATE 86

a

b

c

d

e

f

Back Layout   to   Back Layout

Dolphin Transition

BASIC
ELEMENT   Propulsion of a static position.

STABLE
POSITION   The back layout position with the arms extended above the head was
               described in the albatross transition.

SMOOTH
MOVEMENT   *This transition is truly a complete figure. The body is set in motion
               along a horizontal line by overhead sculling in a headfirst direction. The
               circle begins when the head and shoulders press downward as one unit,
               causing the upper torso to descend. During the circular course, it is required
               that the head, hips, and feet remain on the same circular line, with each
               equidistant from the hub of the circle. The hub is located approximately
               three feet under the head when the swimmer assumes the beginning back
               layout position. During the descent, the body moves through the arms. At
               the bottom of the circle, and until the head reaches the three-quarter mark
               of the circle, sculling is at the hips. The remaining ascent requires control
               of the force of buoyancy. A swimmer may reach the arms to the sides of
               the body and press the palms toward the surface, or the arms may be
               recovered to the original starting position for headfirst sculling. The head
               must surface where it descended before the back layout is completed.*

135

PLATE 87

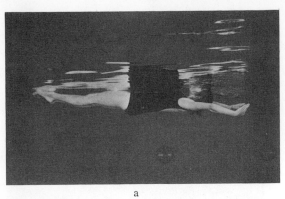

a

b

c

e

d

f

g

h

i

j

k

Back Layout   to   Back Layout

Foot First Dolphin Transition

BASIC
ELEMENT   Propulsion of a static position

STABLE
POSITION   The back layout position was described in ballet leg transition no. 1.

SMOOTH
MOVEMENT   *Like the dolphin transition, this is also truly a complete figure. The body
is set in motion along a horizontal line by foot-first sculling at the hips.
The circle begins as the feet and legs are pressed downward, causing the
pelvis to tilt forward. During the circular course, the feet, hips, and head
must remain on the same circular line, with each equidistant from the hub
of the circle. The hub is located approximately three feet under the feet
when the swimmer assumes the beginning back layout position. During
the descent, the body is propelled by strong mid depth sculling. Scoops
may be used until the feet have passed the three-quarter mark, at which
time sculling overhead assists the control of buoyancy during the ascent.
The feet close the circle at the surface where the descent of the feet had
started. A back layout is then completed.*

PLATE 88

a

b

c

d

e

f

g

h

139

Ballet Leg, Single   to   Axial, Split Variant

Pirouette Transition

BASIC ELEMENTS	Support sculling, body press, airborne leg action, support sculling
STABLE POSITION	The single ballet leg position was described in the ballet leg recovery transition.
SMOOTH MOVEMENT	*Support sculling is at top depth. Movement begins as the head is slightly flexed. A downward press of the shoulder opposite the ballet leg is followed by a torso roll to the stomach. To maintain height during this action, the forearm adjacent to the ballet leg is slipped across the lower abdomen to catch at mid sculling depth. The back is arched and the head hyperex-*

tended. *The ballet leg passes through a moment of abduction followed by adduction. During the body arch, the vertical leg is held in place by the hip extensors. The horizontal leg is raised to the vertical by the hip extensors of that leg. As this occurs, the ballet leg is flexed at both the hip and knee. The leg completes its arc of 180 degrees by a gradual release of the flexors and a strong pull of the extensors. The adductors of both legs hold the thighs close to the mid-body line. During the leg action, sculling is at the mid depth. As the horizontal leg completes its arc, the arms press laterally to bottom depth sculling to stabilize the split axial variant position.*

PLATE 89

a

b

c

d

Ballet Legs Submarine, Double   to   Axial, Split

Gaviata Transition

BASIC
ELEMENTS   Support sculling, body press, airborne leg action, support sculling

STABLE
POSITION   The submarine double ballet legs position was described in the submarine double ballet leg transition no. 1.

SMOOTH
MOVEMENT   *Movement begins as the arms reach to the knees for greater leverage in support sculling. The head is slightly flexed and the chest is pressed upward. Movement toward vertical begins with a down press of the shoulders, resulting in an uplift of the legs. As the torso moves through a pivot roll by means of one shoulder pressing downward and toward the back of the body while the opposite shoulder presses forward, the legs twist with the pivot roll. The chest and head press toward the front of body to establish a vertical line. Only the pelvis tilts forward to enhance the splits. Both legs are eased to the water surface. A gradual release of the hip extensors lowers one leg to the water in front of the swimmer; whereas a gradual release of the hip flexors moves the opposite leg to a horizontal position to the back of the swimmer. The arms support the movement throughout, moving from top depth to mid depth. The gaviata open 180 degrees transition is not shown; however, the legs are opened and begin to move to the water surface just prior to the finish of the pivot roll.*

(Note: In both the gaviata and gaviata open 180 degrees, the back is vertical except for the forward tilt of the pelvis. When the total back is arched during spins or twists, the body will travel off its longitudinal axis.)

Back Layout   to   Back Layout

Circle Shark Transition

BASIC
ELEMENT   Propulsion of a static position

STABLE
POSITION   The back layout position was described in ballet leg transition no. 1.

SMOOTH
MOVEMENT   *Movement begins with a downward press to the side of the body toward which the body is to roll. As the roll is executed, the leg under the body is pressed toward the surface by adduction and the leg at the surface is held there by abduction. The arm adjacent to the submerged side of the*

body begins to scull with the palms facing the feet. The arm at the surface moves along a horizontal arc from its position at the lateral body line to an outstretched position above the head. The upper arm contacts the ear as the head is pressed to the water surface. The shoulders are pressed toward the back of the swimmer as propulsion continues. A circle is traversed at the surface before the back layout is resumed.

PLATE 90

a

b

c

d

e

Back Layout   to   Vertical, Low Water Line

Tailspin Transition

BASIC
ELEMENT   Propulsion of a nearly static position

STABLE
POSITION   The back layout position was described in ballet leg transition no. 1.

SMOOTH
MOVEMENT   *Movement begins with a dowward press to the side of the body toward*
               which the body is to roll. As the roll is executed, the leg under the body
               is pressed toward the surface by adduction and the leg at the surface is
               held there by abduction. The arm adjacent to the submerged side of the
               body begins to scull with the palms facing the feet. The arm at the surface
               moves along a horizontal arc from its position at the lateral body line to
               an outstretched position above the head. The upper arm contacts the ear as
               the head is pressed to the water surface. The shoulders are pressed toward
               the back of the swimmer as propulsion moves the body around one half
               of a circle. After the head has passed the halfway point of the circle, lateral
               flexion of the spine gradually moves the torso deeper. Both arms begin
               to dog-paddle as a means of propulsion. The feet are kept at the surface
               during at least two circles, in which the head is constantly moving closer
               to the hub of the circle. The body is then straightened to a vertical by the
               upper abdominals pressing the shoulders and chest to the plumb line.

PLATE 91

a

b

c

d

e

f

g

Vertical, High Water Line   to   Vertical, Low Water Line

Spinning Transition no. 1

BASIC
ELEMENTS   Support sculling, propulsion, gravity, support sculling

STABLE
POSITION   With the head downward, the body is perpendicular to the water surface.
The weight-bearing parts are in balance with each other so as to decrease
the muscular force necessary to maintain the position. The center of
gravity of the body in this position is toward the front of the body and
toward the head. A water line is maintained between the knees and the
hips by holding the arms in the inverted **T** position while sculling at the
mid depth.

SMOOTH
MOVEMENT   *To spin clockwise 180 degrees while vertical, the left arm pulls or sweeps
toward the front mid line of the body; the right arm sweeps toward the
back mid line. Simultaneously, the left side of the torso is pressed toward the
back of the body as the right side of the torso is pressed toward the front
of the body. To stop the spin at 180 degrees, both forearms rotate inward
as the hands reach the mid-body line. An outward press with palms facing
the pool floor will stop the spinning action. Sculling at bottom depth will
control the speed of descent.*

Vertical, High Water Line   to   Vertical, Low Water Line

Spinning Transition no. 2

BASIC
ELEMENTS   Support sculling, propulsion, gravity

STABLE
POSITION   The beginning vertical was described in spinning transition no. 1.

SMOOTH
MOVEMENT   *To spin clockwise 360 degrees or more while vertical, the left arm pulls
or sweeps toward the front of the body, moving the left hand to the right
lateral line of the body. The right arm sweeps toward the back mid line
and sculls with the hand above the head. As the arms sweep inward, the
torso is pressed to the left. The left shoulder and hip are pressed toward
the back, whereas the right shoulder and hip are pressed toward the front
of the body.*

A complete 360-degree spin is not shown below.

PLATE 92

a

b

c

6

DEVELOPMENTAL MOVEMENTS FOR SYNCHRONIZED SWIMMERS

Though we have constantly stressed that the student aspiring to be a good synchronized swimmer must first be an advanced swimmer of standard strokes, the ability to swim proficiently is only a basic beginning for this sport. A background in speed swimming is highly recommended. Speed develops physical strength and endurance, both of which are essential for competitive synchronized swimming. Often a swimmer's experience in body movement has been limited to standard strokes and everyday movements such as walking, running, and skipping. The synchronized swimmer needs additional exposure to the elements in dance that contribute to the swimming routine and figure performance. Dance training will assist the swimmer in gauging the speed of body movement to fit any rhythmical tempo, and increase interpretive qualities through exposure to authentic movements used in folk dancing, modern dance, and ballet.

The synchronized swimmer is taught specific body movements that are known to produce desired results. These movements are designed for use in the water, where gravity, buoyancy, and water pressure are to be controlled. To prepare the swimmer for these movements, we suggest that training consist of: exercises to stretch and strengthen the stress muscle groups used repeatedly in figure performance; development of isolated movement of body levers; and proper alignment of body parts during stable figure positions.

To achieve a measure of success in these areas, the following developmental movements are prescribed for use in three sections of the pool: deck, trough, and deep water. Several of the deck exercises are performed with a partner so that resistance to movement simulating that of water is made possible. The exercises should be performed slowly by contracting or extending those muscles involved in the movement. Partners apply the force gradually, then rest five seconds and repeat four to six times. The teacher must check to be sure the students are breathing normally.

Because the hands, wrists, forearms, and upper arms are used continuously for either support or propulsion, these levers should be capable of exerting a force against the water sufficient to support approximately fifty pounds of airborne weight. Since this degree of sculling strength is needed specifically in top and mid depth sculling, our deck exercises begin with strength exercises for the shoulders and the arms.

The exercises listed for development of specific body parts progress from moderate to strenuous.

DECK

EXERCISE PLAN FOR THE HANDS, ARMS, AND SHOULDERS

To Strengthen Propulsion Arm Patterns

No. 1

Stand and face partner.

PARTNER A. Place the back of the hands together by rotating the forearms inward, thumbs downward, fingers extended, elbows partially flexed, arms chest high.

PARTNER B. Clasp the hands of A, with palms facing inward, thumbs up, fingers extended.

Force phase:

PARTNER A. Press the hands apart by extending the forearms.

PARTNER B. Add resistance to the movement by pressing the hands together. Repeat three times, then alternate position with partner.

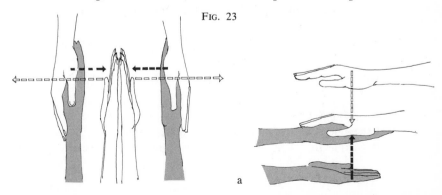

FIG. 23

a   b

No. 2

Stand and face partner. With the elbows near the waist line, hold the upper arms at the lateral body line (along the sides). Flex the forearms until parallel to the floor.

PARTNER A.   Rotate the forearms outward, palms facing upward.

PARTNER B.   Rotate the forearms inward, palms facing downward and over the palms of partner.

Force phase:

PARTNER A.   Press upward by flexing the forearms while keeping the wrists extended.

PARTNER B.   Press downward by extending the forearms while keeping the wrists extended. To allow movement to take place, the downward force should be less than the upward force. Repeat four to six times, alternating positions.

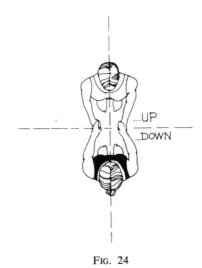

FIG. 24

No. 3

Partners of approximately the same height stand side by side, facing opposite directions.

PARTNER A.   Abduct the upper arm to shoulder height; flex the forearm and hold it upward.

PARTNER B.   Lock elbow with partner, and rotate the arm inward until the forearm is downward.

Force phase:

PARTNER A.   Attempt to lift the upper arm.

PARTNER B.   Add resistance to the upward pressure. Repeat four to six times, alternating position with partner. Exercise both the right and left arms.

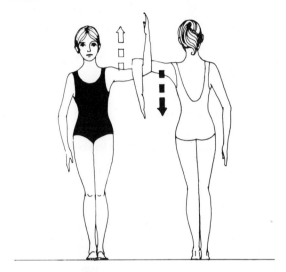

Fig. 25

No. 4

Stand facing partner with right leg forward, weight balanced, arms extended downward, forearms rotated outward, palms facing partner.

Force phase:

Press palms against partner's, slowly moving the arms from the shoulder joint. The movement resembles a slow pendulum swing forward and backward. Do not move the trunk during the action. Repeat the forward and backward arc six times.

Fig. 26

No. 5

Partners stand back to back, arms at shoulder height and to the lateral body line.

PARTNER A. Rotate the arms outward until the palms face the ceiling.

PARTNER B. Rotate the arms inward and place the palms over those of partner.

Force phase:

PARTNER A. Press the arms upward from the shoulders. Do not bend the elbows.

PARTNER B. Press downward to resist the upward movement. As the hands move above the head, reverse the movement, always under resistance. Repeat four to six times. Alternate position with partner.

FIG. 27

To Identify and Strengthen Adduction And Abduction of the Wrist

Partners face each other for this exercise (used in support sculling, top depth at the hips).

PARTNER A. Extend the right arm to the front of the body, flex the forearm until parallel to the chest, palm downward.

PARTNER B. Use both hands, grip the hand and forearm of partner. Add resistance to the wrist movements of partner.

Force phase:

PARTNER A. Move the right hand toward the little-finger side of the hand. This is adduction of the wrist. Now move the hand toward the thumb side of the hand. This is abduction. Slowly repeat wrist action four to six times. Do the same movement with the left hand; alternate position with partner, and repeat.

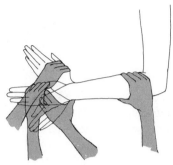

Fig. 28

To Strengthen the Arms and Shoulders

No. 1 (pushups)

Kneel, place hands on floor approximately three feet in front of the knees. Do ten push ups. The greatest movement occurs in the knee and elbow joints. The raising and lowering of the torso counts as one.

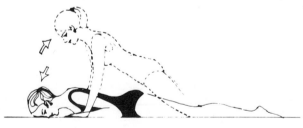

Fig. 29

No. 2

Sit down, legs extended in front of body, adducted (pressed together), ankles extended, toes plantar flexed, hands on floor, forearms rotated outward. Place the heel of each hand close to the hips.

Force phase:

Depress the shoulders, and lift the weight of the torso off the floor. Hold six seconds, repeat four to six times.

FIG. 30

No. 3

(Advanced exercise: modified headstand for the arms and shoulders)

Stand facing the wall. Place hands on floor about eight inches apart, four to five inches from the wall. Flex one leg and extend the other.

Force phase:

Push off with the flexed leg, and lift the body to a vertical position against the wall. Flatten the back, and move the head to vertical alignment. Adduct the legs, extend the ankles, and plantar flex the toes. Keep the legs, torso, and back of the head against the wall. Use a spotter to assist each swimmer. When swimmers show good control, allow them to lower and raise their weight along the vertical line.

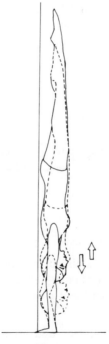

FIG. 31

154

EXERCISE PLAN FOR FLEXIBILITY
OF THE SHOULDER GIRDLE

To Develop a Sequence of Movement
for the Back Pike Somersault

Stand with arms at sides of body. Rotate arms outward. Begin to press the arms backward, then upward, forward, and downward, creating a circle. Rotate the arms inward as they pass vertical above the head. Repeat six times (see Figure 32).

To Develop a Sequence of Movement
for the Forward Pike Somersault

Stand with arms at sides of body. Rotate the arms inward until palms face the back. Press arms backward as far as possible, then rotate outward, lift them over head, rotate inward, and complete the circle. When executing the circle, keep the upper arm as close to the body or head as possible (Figure 33).

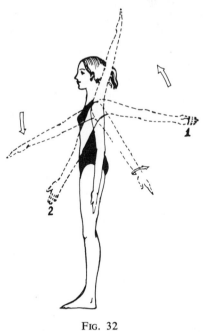

FIG. 32

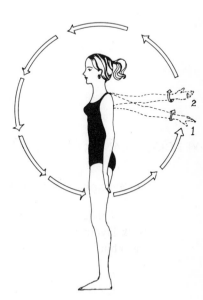

FIG. 33

General Exercise Plan

This is a rhythmic fun exercise, performed to music. Stand with arms extended to the front of the body at shoulder height. While maintaining this height, swing the arms outward and toward the back. Return to the starting position and repeat. Lower the upper arms slightly, and swing the arms outward and backward, again returning to the starting position. As the arms swing backward and downward a fourth time, the hands clap behind the hips before returning to the starting position.

FIG. 34

DECK

EXERCISE PLAN FOR THE UPPER TORSO

To Strengthen the Neck Muscles

This exercise is devised for proper positioning of the head in the front or back layout and vertical. Stand holding hands at the base of the skull and tuck the chin.

Force phase:
Press the head backward against the hands as the hands are pressed against the head. Hold six seconds. Repeat four times (see Figure 35).

To Strengthen and Identify the Shoulder Press

This represents secondary propulsion; the torso is pressed from horizontal to vertical. Partners sit back to back, legs flexed, feet on floor, hands resting on knees, head flexed.

Force phase:

Contract the upper abdominals, followed by a backward press of the torso, causing partners to press backward against each other. Hold the press six seconds or until one partner is pushed away. Repeat four times (see Figure 36).

To Identify the Pivot Roll Press of the Shoulders

The pivot roll press is used in the catalina, gaviata, and pirouette. Partners sit back to back, torso erect, legs extended in front of the body, legs adducted, ankles extended, toes plantar flexed, hands resting on floor.

Force phase:

Rotate upper torso, and press against partner's opposite shoulder. As one unit, turn the head with the shoulder press. Hold the rotation, and press for six seconds. Release, and press the other shoulder. This exercise is bilateral and develops a pivot in either direction. However, usually the pivot roll is executed to the left (Figure 37).

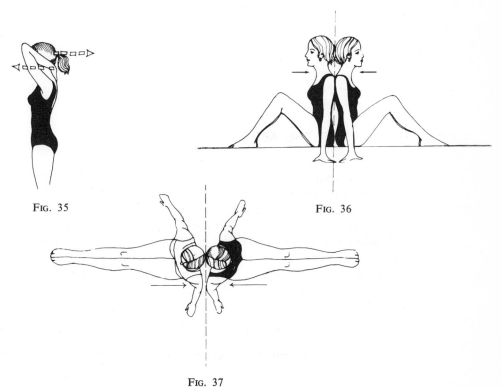

FIG. 35

FIG. 36

FIG. 37

To Isolate the Upper Torso Arch

The upper torso arch is executed in all walkout figures. Stand, upper arms extended shoulder high, elbows at 115 degrees to the upper arms.

Force phase:

Contract the upper back muscles, moving the chest upward and the shoulders backward. Let the head lie back on the shoulders. Move the arms with the shoulder and chest action. Repeat slowly four times, always beginning at vertical alignment.

Fig. 38

DECK

EXERCISE PLAN FOR THE ABDOMINAL MUSCLES

The abdominal muscles are used repeatedly in alignment of body parts during the stable positions that appear in chapter 3. The lower rectus abdominus is highly activated when the pelvis is tilted, whereas the upper rectus abdominus is involved primarily when there is movement of the upper torso.[1] The abdominals perform in two different ways: when they *stretch* while controlling a movement the action is called pliometric, whereas the *contraction* phase is referred to as miometric.[2] The following exercises will help strengthen the abdominal muscles.

[1] C. Walter, Ph. D., M. Partridge, B.S. *American Journal of Physical Medicine,* 1957, pp. 259–68.

[2] William Hillcourt, *Your Guide to Fitness* (New York: Golden Press, 1967).

To Strengthen Miometric Action of the Lower Abdominals
(curl up and sit up modifications)

MODERATE EXERCISES

No. 1

Repeat four to six times.

    a. Lie on the back, knees flexed at forty-five degrees, pelvis tilted backward and upward until the lower back touches the deck. Hold this position for six seconds.

    b. Same exercise except legs and ankles are extended, adducted, and toes plantar flexed.

No. 2

Lie on the back, knees flexed to chest; feet traverse a large circle in alternating action. The pelvis is held in a backward tilt so that the back is flat (bicycle exercise).

No. 3

Lie on the back, legs extended. Raise legs to ninety degrees; lower slowly to starting position.

STRENUOUS EXERCISES

No. 1

Lie on back, legs flexed at ninety degrees at the knees. Arms at sides. Curl the head to the chest, and raise the torso to an upright position. Slowly return to the starting position.

No. 2

Same as no. 1. Repeat the same exercise with the hands behind the neck and the elbows held forward. To increase the difficulty of no. 1 and no. 2, move the heels close to the buttocks.

Fig. 39

No. 3

Same as no. 1. Lie on the back, arms at side, and legs outstretched on deck. Raise the legs and arms at the same time until a **V** is formed. Slowly return to the starting position.

Fig. 40

No. 4

Same as no. 1. Lie on the back, arms at side, palms down, and knees flexed to the chest. Raise the buttocks until the last lumbar vertebra comes off the deck approximately five inches (reverse curl, Figure 41).

No. 5

Same as no. 1. The most difficult abdominal exercise is known as a basket hang. Since the pool area is seldom equipped with a horizontal bar, the end of the diving board can be used instead. Beginning in a tread-water position, the swimmer should reach up and grasp the sides of the board, facing the end of the board. The body should hang extended. Draw the knees to the chest until the pelvis tilts up and backward. Hold for six seconds, and slowly uncurl to the extended position. Repeat four to six times (Figure 42).

Fig. 41

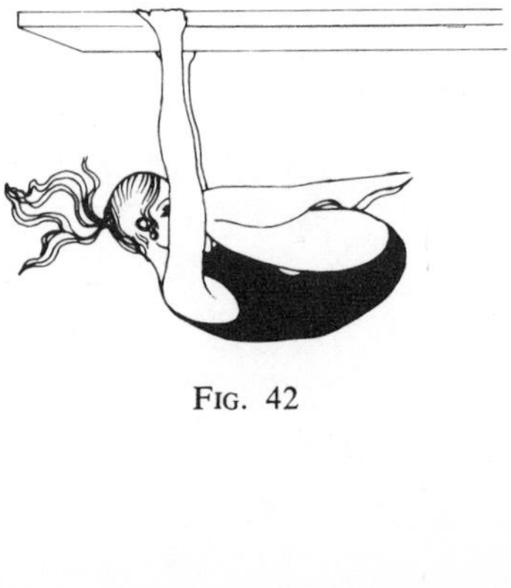

Fig. 42

To Strengthen the Miometric Action of the Upper Abdominals

No. 1

Lie on the back, flex the knees, and have a partner hold the feet. Repeat the first strenuous exercise previously listed.

No. 2

Lie on the back, arms at side, knees flexed to ninety degrees. Curl the upper torso forward until the seventh cervical vertebra is off the deck approximately seven inches (trunk curl).

Fig. 43

No. 3

Lie on the back, repeat exercise no. 2, with the addition of twisting until a shoulder is in line with an opposite knee.

POSITIONS AND MOVEMENT OF THE PELVIS

To teach and to learn figure transitions, both the teacher and the swimmer will benefit from knowledge of pelvic action. Because pelvic movement and position significantly effect alignment and balance of other body parts, control of this area is a constant challenge. For example, the pelvis is tilted up and backward during tuck and pike positions, whereas it moves forward and rotates during the execution of the split axial. Only a forward tilt is desirable in the reverse split axial. All verticals, high or low, require the pelvis held at mid center along the plumb line. Many swimmers describe the mid line position as a feeling of tucking the lower end of the spine into the pelvic girdle.

Because the pelvis absorbs the weight of the airborne legs, its control is subject to the strength of the abdominal, back, and hip muscles. Because of lack of strength, it is common for a beginner synchronizer, when attempting to support a vertical position, to hold the pelvis in one of three incorrect positions: completely arched (tilted forward); arched with the legs piked at the hips; or tilted backward, causing the swimmer to lean onto the stomach.

In the artists illustrations, those muscles capable of moving the pelvis are shown by lines. Those lines extending from the rib cage to the front of the pelvis (abdominals) are responsible for a backward tilt, whereas those lines from the lower back to the pelvis move the pelvis forward. The diagonal lines are those muscles that attach to the pelvis and legs. These are capable of rotating the pelvis and moving it either forward or backward. Note: The pelvis usually follows the direction of the legs or leg.

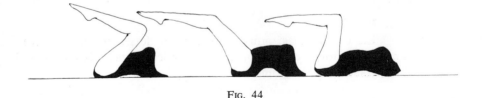

FIG. 44

DECK

EXERCISE PLAN FOR THE MUSCLES OF THE BACK

Synchronized swimmers must have a flexible back, and the muscles attached to the spine must be strong. These factors are brought into action during the execution of the swordfish, hightower, and castle figures.

To Strengthen the Back and Hip Extensors

Mats or a terry towel should be used to protect the pelvic area of the swimmer.

MODERATE

Lie on the stomach, arms at the sides.

Force phase:

a. Raise the head and chest off the floor by contracting the upper back muscles. Hold for six seconds. Return to the starting position, and repeat four times.
b. Raise both legs off the floor by contracting the hip extensors. Hold six seconds; return to the starting position; repeat four times.
c. Raise both legs, head, and chest off the floor, and hold six seconds. Return to the starting position, and repeat four times.

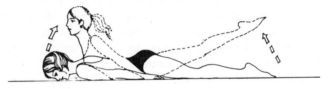

FIG. 45

To Strengthen the Back Extensors

STRENUOUS

This exercise is performed with a partner who holds the legs of the swimmer. The swimmer must lie prone at the edge of the pool. Place the hands on the lip of the trough to support the upper torso. Move the body forward out over the water until free to flex at the hips. Place the hands behind the head and lower the trunk into the water.

Force phase:

Lift the torso to a horizontal position, and hold four seconds; then, slowly flex at the hips, moving the torso to the water. Repeat the raising and lowering four times. To complete the exercise, catch the trough with the hands, and direct the partner to release the legs. Slide the body headfirst into the water.

Fig. 46

EXERCISE FOR FLEXIBILITY OF THE SPINE

To Strengthen Hyperextension of the Spine

PARTNER A.   Lie prone on deck, arms at side, palms up.
PARTNER B.   Facing partner, kneel, straddle her legs, and hold her wrists.

Force phase:

As partner A arches the back and elevates the chest off the floor, partner B carefully pulls the arms toward her body.

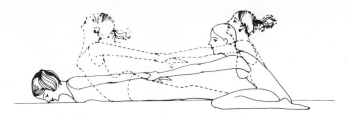

Fig. 47

EXERCISE FOR THE HORIZONTAL LAYOUT POSITION

To Strengthen Posture Alignment of the Body

This exercise requires three persons.

PARTNER A.   Lie on back, arms at sides.

PARTNER B.   Squat at the head end of partner A, and hold the hands under her neck.

PARTNER C.   Squat at the foot end of partner A and hold the hands under her heels.

Force phase:

Partner A gives the command to lift. Partners B and C lift the body of partner A off the floor approximately eight to ten inches. Be sure the person being lifted is considerably lighter in weight than those doing the lifting, who must bend their knees to lift in order to prevent back strain. Keep the body and arms level during the upward and downward action.

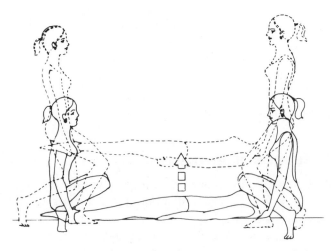

Fig. 48

DECK

EXERCISE PLAN FOR THE LEGS

To Strengthen the Knee Extensors

PARTNER A.   Sit on the pool deck with legs at pool edge, feet in the water.

PARTNER B.   In the water holding the ankles of partner.

   Force phase:

PARTNER A.   Begin to straighten the knees and lift B out of the water. Hold for six seconds. Release, and repeat four times.

To Stretch the Knee and Hip Extensors

Sit with legs extended in front of body

Force phase:

Flex the ankles and extend the knees toward the floor. Reach forward and pull the toes toward the body while pressing the torso to the thighs. Release, and repeat six times.

FIG. 49

To Stretch the Hip Extensors

PARTNER A.   Lie prone, resting upper torso on forearms. Adduct the legs.

PARTNER B.   Kneel and straddle the legs of partner; place hands on her thighs, just above the knees.

   Force phase:

PARTNER A.   Lift the knees off the floor. Hold for six seconds.

PARTNER B.   Exert a relatively small amount of downward pressure on the legs. Repeat four times, then alternate position with partner.

FIG. 50

To Adduct the Legs

This is used in the layout and double ballet legs. Sit in an upright position with hands on floor. Face partner and move close enough so that the legs may overlap when extended forward.

PARTNER A.   Adduct and extend legs toward partner.

PARTNER B.   Abduct (hold feet twelve inches apart) from ankles to knees; the legs must touch the outside of partner's legs.

Force phase:

PARTNER A.   Press the legs outward (abduct).

PARTNER B.   Press the legs inward (adduct). Hold the pressure against the legs for six seconds. Repeat four times; alternate position with partner.

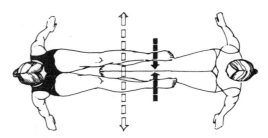

FIG. 51

To Strengthen Adduction and Abduction of the Thighs

Sit with legs flexed and slightly apart. Cross the forearms and grasp the knees.

Force phase:

Press the knees together, using the adductors of the legs, while pressing the hands apart. Hold the force six seconds. Reverse, and press the knees apart, using the abductors of the legs, while pressing the hands together.

FIG. 52

To Develop Flexibility of the Knees, Ankles, and Toes

Sit with knees and ankles flexed, back erect, hands on floor.

Force phase:

This is a rhythmical exercise. On count one, extend the knees and ankles and relax the toes. Continue to flex and extend the legs and feet twenty times. Use music for count and tempo.

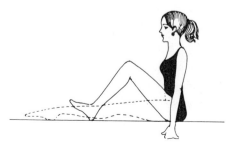

FIG. 53

DECK

STRENGTH AND STRETCHING EXERCISE PLAN FOR THE FEET

The position of the feet is important to the aesthetic appearance of all positions and transitions used in figures. The ankles should be extended and the toes plantar flexed.

To Manipulate the Ankles and Feet

a. Stand and contract the feet by raising the arches off the floor. Hold six seconds. Repeat four times.

b. Stand and raise just the big toe, keeping other toes on the floor; then, lower the big toe and raise the others.

c. Stand and raise the heels off the floor as high as possible. Walk around the pool on tip toes.

d. Begin standing on the toes, let one foot down by shifting the weight to that foot. Follow by shifting the weight to the toes of the other foot and slowly lower it to the floor. Increase the speed of the shifting weight until performing a prancing movement. Be sure the thighs are held parallel and the knees move directly forward. Do not permit the hips to sway or the ankles to buckle outward.

e. Practice picking up pencils with the toes.

f. Stand facing a wall with hands against the wall. Sway the torso toward the wall until the nose touches the wall. Repeat while standing approximately three feet from the wall.

TENSION EXERCISES FOR FLEXIBILITY

Important to the synchronized swimmer is the ability to perform tension positions without evidence of muscular strain. Those positions to which we refer are:

1. The split axial
2. The split axial variant
3. The back pike
4. The tuck axial
5. The reverse split axial

The authors recommend Gerda Alexander's *eutonie* method for learning these tension positions.[3] This method has been scientifically researched and is capsuled here by saying that it requires relaxation of those muscles to be stretched, followed by an increase in the stretch, followed by relaxation, in that order. The exercises must be performed slowly so that the muscle fibers do not tear. Those muscles that resist stretching are called the antagonistic muscles. Although these muscles will pain during the stretching, daily practice of the tension positions will increase the elasticity of the muscles, resulting in a decrease in pain. Through practice, the synchro swimmer should attain the ability to execute all the tension positions shown here.

TENSION-TESTING EXERCISES FOR FLEXIBILITY

FIG. 54   FIG. 55

[3] Margaret C. Brown and Betty K. Sommer, *Movement Education: Its Evolution and a Modern Approach* (Reading, Mass.: Addison-Wesley Publishing Company, 1969).

Fig. 56

Fig. 57

Fig. 58

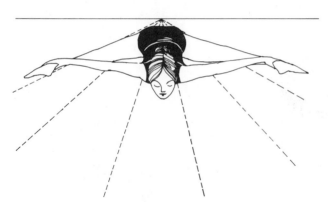

Fig. 59

Fig. 60

Fig. 61

Fig. 62

EXERCISES AT THE TROUGH FOR STABLE POSITIONS

Exercises performed in the water at the trough are highly recommended because the body can be supported while isolated movements and specific positions are practiced.

To Develop the Tuck Axial

Face the wall and hold the trough. Tuck the legs, lie on back in water. Draw the thighs to the chest, flex the spine, protract the shoulders, and bring the head to a flexed position.

Force phase:

Press the shoulders downward in the water as the abdominals contract. Roll the body toward its back until the lower legs are vertical to the water surface. Hold the position and the breath for six seconds. Recover by releasing the hands and completing the backward somersault until the feet are downward and under the hips. Stand up, and repeat the exercise four times. (The teacher may need to assist the swimmer in finding the vertical position of the lower legs.)

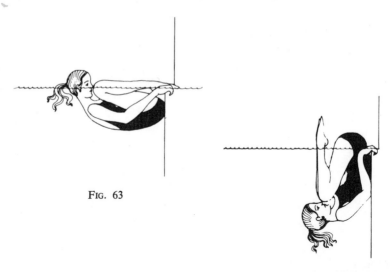

FIG. 63

FIG. 64

To Develop the Double Ballet Legs Position

Face the pool wall, hold the trough, lie on back with both legs vertically extended upward from the water surface. Do not press the calf of the legs against the wall.

Force phase:

Flex the knee joints without moving the thighs. Keep the legs adducted, ankles extended, and toes plantar flexed. Follow by extending the knees. Repeat slowly ten times.

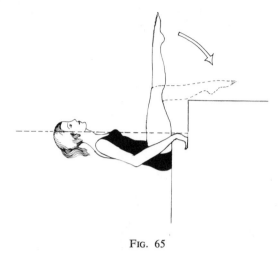

Fig. 65

To Develop a Vertical

Face the pool wall, hold the trough, and assume a double ballet legs position.
Force phase:
With the water line above the knees, begin by slightly flexing the head; contract the upper abdominals, and with the back muscles, press the shoulders downward in the water. Press through until the back and head are against the wall. Stretch the legs from the hip socket, adduct the legs, and rotate the thighs outward as the hip extensors contract. The ankles are extended and the toes plantar flexed. Be sure the anatomical markings of the head, body, and legs are in line. Those markings are the little toe, the ankle bone, the knee joint, the hip bone, the shoulder, and the ear. Recover by pressing the chest and head toward the surface as the body flexes at the hips. Return to the surface and repeat slowly four times. Hold the trough throughout.

To Develop Alignment of the Front Pike Vertical, Forward Split Vertical, and Vertical Variant

Face the pool wall, hold the trough, assume a double ballet legs position.
Force phase:
Repeat the torso descent as described in the exercise to develop a vertical. Following the establishment of the vertical, slowly lengthen the extensors of the hips, moving the legs to a horizontal position at the water surface. Keep the back and head straight, along the wall of the pool. This is the front pike position. Continue by slowly contracting the right leg extensors, raising that leg to vertical.

This position is the forward split vertical. Follow by slowly flexing the left knee and hip joints, placing the left foot inside the thigh of the vertical right leg. This is the vertical variant position. Hold each position for four counts. Recover by flexing both legs and moving away from the wall.

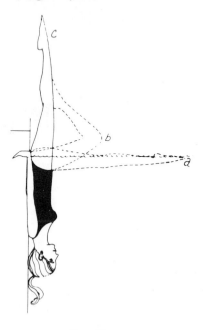

FIG. 66

a.   Front pike
b.   Vertical variant
a. and c.   Forward split vertical

To Develop the Split Axial

Begin in four feet of water. Assume a front layout position on the water surface. By means of arm propulsion and a downward chest press, in that order, move to the front pike vertical, placing the hands on the pool floor. Flex one leg at the knee and then extend it to the back of the body, being sure to keep the foot of that leg at the water surface. Split the legs to maximum. Let the pelvis tilt forward to enhance the position of the legs. Keep the head and upper torso in vertical alignment. Balance the split axial for six seconds. Recover by tucking both legs, and bring the shoulders to the water surface.

To Develop the Split Axial Variant

Begin in four feet of water. Assume a front layout position on the water surface. Move to the front pike position by means of arm propulsion and a downward chest press, in that order. Place the hands on the pool floor. Flex one leg at the knee and extend it to the back of the body, keeping the foot of that leg at the water surface. Flex the second leg and place the foot along the inside of the leg that is extended to the back of the body. Contract the back muscles, moving the head and shoulders toward the leg that is extended to the back of the body. Hold the spinal arch for six seconds. Recover by releasing the arch through the shoulders, allowing buoyancy to surface the body feet-first until afloat, horizontally, at the water surface.

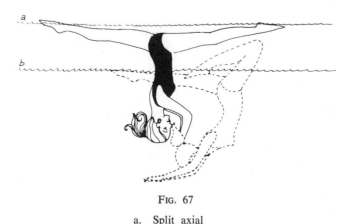

FIG. 67

a. Split axial
b. Axial variant

EXERCISE PLAN AT THE TROUGH
FOR THE HANDS, ARMS, AND SHOULDERS

To Develop Strength for Propulsion and/or Support Sculling

Assume a back layout, toes touching the trough.

Force phase:

Keep the body horizontal while executing twenty scoops. The arms begin at the hips, are rotated outward, and then pressed laterally to an overhead extension. The arms slowly recover to the hips to repeat the force phase. When the body is vertical, this movement, with a slight variation (weaving the forearms and hands across the lateral line of the body during the scoop) is called a feather press.

FIG. 68

DEEP WATER EXERCISE PLAN
FOR THE ARMS AND SHOULDERS

To Develop Strength for Support Sculling at Mid Depth

With back to the wall of the pool, hold the upper arms along the side of the body; flex the forearms—hands in line with the forearms, palms toward the surface.

Force phase:

Scull in this position forcing the body downward in the water. Keep the legs, head, and torso straight along the pool wall. Scull the body position to the floor of the pool and remain there for six seconds. Recover for another breath, and repeat four times.

To Develop Strength for the Feather Press of the Arms

Position the body vertically in the water.

Force phase:

Begin with the arms in the **T** position and feather press (scoop) toward the pool floor. Hold the vertical; descend to the ankles. Quickly recover the arms to mid sculling depth; move them to the **T** position, lateral line and repeat the feather press. A swimmer should be able to execute at least three feather press patterns before coming to the surface for a breath. Twenty feather presses should be practiced, counting only those that truly send the body feet-first along a plumb line; those presses in which the body travels off its center should not be counted.

Fig. 69

To Develop Strength for Mid Depth Sculling

Position the body in a forward split vertical.

Force phase:

Scull at mid depth for ten seconds, keeping the water line nearly at the bathing-suit leg line.

A POTPOURRI OF DEVELOPMENTAL MOVEMENT

To insure the development of strength, flexibility, and a feeling for the correct alignment of stable positions, the teacher should require daily practice of each of the following exercises.

a.   Support sculling of airborne legs, stationary, and feet first.

b.   Holding of tension-testing positions on deck and in the water.

c.   Propulsion arm movements (scoops and pulls).

d.   Propulsion leg movements in the form of races: flutter kicking on the back, left and right side, and stomach; races to be repeated within a set time limit.

e.   Egg beater kicking for a set time limit—three minutes recommended.

f.   Deck exercises for strength and flexibility.

g.   All forms of sculling races.

Because a number of books are available on the subject of exercise, we have confined our developmental movements to those most pertinent to synchronized swimming. We believe that many of the muscular actions used by the synchronized swimmer are more readily understood when taught on deck before experimentation in the water. Also, we believe that through these deck exercises the swimmer is able to associate the name of the movement with the movement itself, thus increasing her knowledge of body mechanics. For example, the isolated movements of inward and outward rotation of the forearm are not used frequently in daily activities, and yet these movements are indispensable and repeated over and over in both propulsion and support sculling. Deck and trough exercises hasten the learning of stable positions because the head, torso, and legs can be moved to the proper position without loss of support.

We believe that when the synchronized swimmer understands the mechanics of sculling and is able to muscularly control the head and pelvis, the remaining biomechanics of the figures will be simplified. Practice may then give emphasis to the building of strength and flexibility, and to the improvement of timing. Remedial teaching (the correction of basic sculling and body line) will not absorb the greatest share of teaching time. For these reasons, we stress the value to be gained in figure performance from deck and trough exercises that are readily transferred to deep water performance.

7

COACHING THE COMPETITIVE SYNCHRONIZED SWIMMER

The coach is the primary person responsible for keeping the synchronized swimming program alive and vibrant in the world of sports. In the public school class or the athletic club, the coach creates the structure of the program, selects the methods to use in developing the swimmer, motivates swimmer participation, sets goals, directs the water show, and conducts clinics, meets, and demonstrations for other coaches, officials, swimmers, and the general public. The coach must know the essential elements of physiology and physics to give intelligent guidance in this sport. In short, the multiplicity involved requires reading, film study, planning, experience—all combined with a personality that will cause both the artistic and athletic potential of each synchronized swimmer to blossom.

In the high school and college activities programs during the nineteen forties and early fifties, synchronized swimming was influenced by the Esther Williams screen spectaculars, and was better known as water ballet. Until stunt figures penetrated the "art" emphasis, the teacher was primarily concerned with writing a routine that had great audience appeal. Emphasis was given to costuming, scenery, staging, and special effects.

Present-day teaching-coaching of the sport of synchronized swimming requires specialization in techniques used in the figures and a scientific approach to related aquatic movements. Today, the emphasis is to develop individual skills. Loop films of all the figures listed in the AAU handbook are available for rent or purchase. A national magazine containing pictures and articles is circulated to subscribers around the world.[1] Knowledgeable coaches who have made an in-depth study of the figures are conducting training clinics in the United States, Canada, South America, Europe, and Asia. Today, competitive synchronized swimming, which is recognized as a sport for girls and women around the world, deserves a place in the Olympic games.

The coach of competitive synchronized swimming is responsible for creating a training atmosphere in which progress is assured for each swimmer. Emphasis is placed on effective use of the pool time, adapting swimming strokes to music, developing the schooled figures, coaching the routine, and conditioning the swimmer. To attain some degree of success in these areas, the coach must have a vast reservoir of knowledge and skill pertinent to this sport. Hopefully, the in-depth study presented here will impart much of the knowledge necessary for coaching skill development.

TRAINING METHODS

Group Workouts

Following tryouts for the class or club of synchronized swimmers, the coach embarks upon a training program that will challenge the unskilled student as well as the more advanced. All levels of swimmers will benefit from basic group workouts through which camaraderie is nourished. Stroking and speed sculling races provide an excellent point of departure. For maximum use of pool time and space, a class of twenty to thirty members should swim the warm-up laps in waves of four or five abreast. One direction of travel is indicated by the black lines, and the swim lanes accommodate those swimming in the opposite direction, It is advisable to prepare tapes of music for warm-up stroking well ahead of each class period. We recommend the use of a variety of rhythms and tempos. Be sure the music has a strong downbeat (one that will assist both coach and swimmer in keeping a rhythmical cadence): "Pull, kick, glide," for the breast and side stroke; "lift and catch" for the crawl and back stroke. Approximately eight minutes of music will provide rhythm for the swimming of twenty laps, the recommended minimum distance for each class warm-up. At the conclusion of stroke swimming, a brief rest period is given while teams are organized for relay sculling races. All types of sculling are included and begin with a layout position in the water.

Schooled Figure Practice

The selection of figures to be practiced is often determined by the levels of competition offered by the AAU. To compete in the figure event, swimmers must develop those compulsory figures that comply with the recognized levels

---

[1] Dawn Bean, "Synchro-Info." 11902 Red Hill Avenue, Santa Ana, California.

of competition. The first level encompasses age group, junior olympic, and novice meets in which the kip, dolphin, and somersub, plus two optionals of any difficulty, are performed. The second level, junior association, consists of four compulsory figures with two optionals of any difficulty. The third level includes senior association, junior national, and senior national meets in which six figures are drawn from a list of thirty compulsory schooled figures. To prepare for entry in all levels of figure competition, the swimmer must develop proficiency in the execution of approximately thirty-seven different schooled figures.

To enhance class organization, post the order for the practice of the swimming routines. Those swimmers who are not using the music must divide their time so that they participate in each of the following activities:

1. Practice stable positions and sculling transitional patterns against the wall at the shallow or deep end.
2. Work with a partner on figure transitions.
3. Participate in developmental exercises.
4. Walk through the routine with team members.
5. Work with a dance instructor on deck movements and arm actions used in the routine.

The format for each class may be varied to include group participation in figure repeats. This activity is planned by the coach and directed by the use of an underwater speaker. The coach announces the schooled figures, or parts thereof, to be repeated and counts aloud in the rhythmic time frame desired for each transition within the figure. The group responds in unison. We refer to the activity as repetitive figure training. For the beginning synchronized swimmer, it is most effective to conduct this form of training at the shallow end, where the swimmer may use the wall or floor. For the more advanced swimmer, sessions of this nature conducted in deep water will increase strength through the arms and shoulders while building endurance. Also effective is the swimming of a standard routine, one that includes a variety of skills. Such a routine is so constructed that twenty to thirty swimmers may participate at a time. From these suggestions it should be clearly understood that the objective for each class workout is to make maximum use of the pool time to insure swimmer progress.

ADAPTING SWIMMING STROKES

Form

Because the name *synchronized swimming* implies togetherness during aquatic movement, the coach must require identical stroke patterns. Form is, therefore, of primary importance. The swimmer will readily learn form from observing a demonstration accompanied by an explanation of the arm action: the size of the pattern, the recovery, the entrance of the hands in the water, and the timing of the total action. Equally important is the action of the legs. The coach must explain that an identical kicking pattern performed in the same relative time frame is required of all the swimmers. Because the kicking action is often the greatest source of driving power in synchronized swimming, it must produce a constant rate of propulsion. The continuous drive must be regulated so that swimmers cover the same distance with each kick; while stroking, the objective is to keep the space between the swimmers relatively constant. Although the standard breast stroke and the side stroke employ a glide within the pattern (a glide is a period of rest during which no action occurs), synchronized swimmers must fill the glide with flutter kicking. The music determines the tempo for the stroke, and that tempo is utilized by both arm and leg action. No attempt is made to synchronize the flutter kick of each leg; however, the scissor and modified wedge kicks utilize a downbeat.

Stroke Dynamics

Stroking may be described as slow, with accentuated smoothness; moderate, with perfection in pattern; or rapid and crisp, with power. In each case, propulsion should be constant, devoid of spurts of speed. The slow and smooth stroke causes a slight ripple as the body glides across the water. The kick is powerful but not necessarily rapid. The legs are under the surface so that no splash is evidenced. The moderate stroke utilizes less time for each pattern, as the swimmer travels with increased speed. The rapid and crisp stroke displays power in the driving kick, and the arm action appears to cut both the air and the water. Because stroke dynamics are variable, swimmers should be encouraged to execute that which complements the mood and tempo of the music.

DEVELOPMENT OF SCHOOLED FIGURES

Basic Aqua Data

It is folly to attempt to coach the figures devoid of basic aqua science. An empirical approach belabors both coaching and swimmer development. For information regarding aqua science (the positive buoyancy factor of the immersed body and the location of the center of gravity in various body positions used in synchronized swimming), refer to chapters 10, 11, and 12 in the text, *Synchronized Swimming,* by George Rackham. Various experiments and illustrations are presented there to assist the reader in understanding laws of physics related to the human body in water.

Communication with the Swimmer

The alert teacher must be prepared to meet the challenges that accompany the teaching of schooled figures. To overcome the first problem of communication, use descriptive words that always relate to the same specific movement or position. This will help to establish complete communication between the swimmer and the coach. For example, the swimmer must be oriented to the directional changes that take place from deck to water. It will be necessary to identify upward, downward, top, and bottom; for when the swimmer is vertical in the water, directions are reversed from those on deck. To further explain: while standing, we naturally extend the arms overhead when the command is to reach up. Likewise, we are accustomed to gravity pulling us feet-first to the earth, like a magnet. When vertical in the water, head downward, the swimmer must stretch the arms toward the feet to reach up. Up is toward the surface. Gravity, although it appears to have less force, is pulling the swimmer headfirst, whereas buoyancy is pressing the body to the surface. When teaching the twists or spins from the deck, the body must move counterclockwise if the identical movement in an aquatic vertical is to move clockwise. As we walk along on deck, we swing our legs forward toward the front of our body and then balance. However, in the water there are a preponderance of figure transitions that require us to swing our legs backward and balance. The authors refer to this form of communication as programming the swimmer. When the swimmer understands the terminology and responds favorably, the coach may feel the key to teaching science has been successfully applied. (The terms most frequently used in coaching figures are listed in chapter 5.)

Coaching Aids

Loop films, descriptions of movement, a demonstration by a swimmer whose expertise is outstanding, and the use of a jointed cardboard mannequin will aid the coach in her development of good figure performers.[2] We also recommend that the coach and swimmer participate in clinics where new and different ways of performing are analyzed by experts in the field.

Individual Instruction

Each swimmer requires individual instruction. When working with one swimmer, in a sense the coach becomes a physician concerned with the trouble areas in execution. Usually developmental exercises are prescribed to help alleviate the problems. Specific land and water exercises are most effective. (Refer to chapter 6 for what we consider developmental exercises.)

Verbal Corrections

When coaching the competitor, it is wise to correct one error at a time

---

[2] Wilbur Luick, *Authorized training and coaching films of synchronized swimming skills.* Jole Company, P.O. Box 95150, San Jose, California. Also Frances Jones and Joyce Lindeman, *Twelve loop films and wall charts of basic positions.* Champions on Film, 745 State Circle, Ann Arbor, Michigan.

so that the swimmer may concentrate on making a single change. We recommend emphasis be given to body line, followed by sculling at the correct depth that corresponds to the body position. Because sculling in the relative plane and at the correct depth is dependent upon the accuracy of the design, these two elements are so interrelated they are inseparable. For example, when the design is not the prescribed line, poor balance causes an overload on the sculling action that results in a struggle to find balance and to support the position. Usually such a struggle causes the body to travel when it should remain stationary. The coach needs experience to make an effective and quick appraisal of the body line, and if a fault is present, to know how to remedy it. Experienced coaches often teach the arm positions for stable positions in the belief that if the arms are sculling in the proper place, the body position will be correct.

Positioning the Head

We believe the head is the key component in the anatomy of the total schooled figure. It can be the primary factor in establishing balance, or the cause of both desirable and undesirable movement. For example, transitions are executed with greater ease and fluidity when the head is carried in the position that augments the movement of the torso. Stable positions cannot be stable unless the head is in the proper position corresponding to the alignment of the remainder of the trunk.

In this sport, there are three basic positions in which the head may be carried. When it is in line with the shoulders, its weight of ten to twelve pounds assists the swimmer in stretching vertical and horizontal lines as each line appears during the figure sequence. When the head is pressed forward toward the chest, it aids in rounding the back, whereas hyperextension of the head increases the body arch. Because the weight of the head is farthest from the center of gravity of the body, a slight tilt of that weight away from the plumb line greatly affects body balance and is the cause of motion. Therefore, when coaching vertical positions, the head must be in line to remain stationary. Caution the swimmer to move the head very slowly toward or away from the plumb line to augment desirable movement and axial positions.

Since effective coaching of the figure design involves the use of the part-to-whole method (the simple body position, top depth support sculling, primary propulsion followed by secondary propulsion), we suggest the coach begin with the position of the head assumed by the swimmer during her performance. Although horizontal and vertical stable positions require a truly extended plumb line head position, transitions that involve movement from horizontal to vertical require that the head be carried in a slightly flexed position. Note: Both the dolphin and foot-first dolphin figures are considered transitions because the body line does change from horizontal to axial and returns to horizontal. These transitions are unique in that they appear to resemble a static position. However, the spine is moved from extension to hyperextension, causing the head and shoulders to move as one unit. Although we would expect the head to hyperextend as one lever to complement the axial position, it moves as the result of hyperextension of the thoracic portion of the spine.

To achieve the correct head position for a horizontal or vertical torso, the muscles of the neck must be "educated" to press the head toward the back, keeping the chin level, until the ears are in line with the lateral line of the shoulders. This does not mean to nod the head. One cue to help the swimmer align her head properly is the use of visual focus. When in a back layout, the swimmer should make eye contact straight up at the ceiling. If the swimmer is able to see the feet while in the back layout, her head is too far forward (flexed). During practice of verticals, the pool wall is used as a visual marker. Position the swimmer so that the front of the body faces the pool wall. If, when in a vertical, the swimmer looks at the pool floor directly below her, unequivocally her head will be hyperextended.

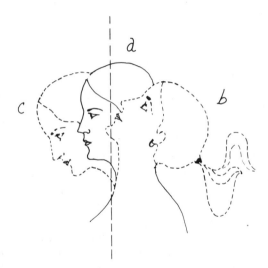

FIG. 70   The three head positions used in stunt figures

a. Extension (plumb line)
b. Hyperextension
c. Flexion

Postural Compensations

Misuse of the head alignment forces postural compensations among other parts of the body. Once a swimmer becomes accustomed to the incorrect posture, it is difficult to break the habit of holding that position. To aid the teacher in detecting postural compensations caused by an incorrect head position, the following information is offered. The left column lists the stable positions in which the head is required to be in line with the torso as shown in plumb line extension A. The far right column lists common postural compensations resulting from the head being flexed toward the chest.

Stable Position	Fault	Probable Postural Compensation
Back layout	Head flexed	Rounded shoulders, sunken hips
Front layout	Head flexed	Protracted shoulders, legs piked
Back tuck, open	Head flexed	Torso angled deep in water
Ballet leg	Head flexed	Mid section sinking, abdominals overloaded
Ballet legs, double	Head flexed	Low hips; back of shoulders rounded, causing body to rock forward
Vertical	Head flexed	Body traveling toward the back
Vertical, front pike variant	Head flexed	Over-piked and falling toward the back
Vertical, forward split	Head flexed	Traveling toward the back
Axial, reverse split	Head flexed	Traveling toward the back
Axial, split	Head flexed	Loss of balance and traveling

When coaching the stable verticals, the most frequent correction is to rid the swimmer of a hyperextended head. This incorrect position of the head is readily detected through the appearance of the total body line when the verticals are practiced in deep water. The far right column lists the postural compensations resulting from the head at rest on the back of the shoulders.

Stable Position	Fault	Probable Postural Compensation
Back layout	Hyperextended head	Chest protruding, head and feet sinking
Back tuck, open	Hyperextended head	Neck protruding, chin not level
Ballet leg, single	Hyperextended head	Neck protruding, chin not level
Vertical	Hyperextended head	Back arched, traveling and falling on stomach
Vertical, front pike	Hyperextended head	Back arched, pelvic tilt, legs over-piked
Vertical, forward split	Hyperextended head	Falling on the stomach
Axial, reverse split	Hyperextended head	Total back arched, traveling toward the back of body
Axial, split	Hyperextended head	Back arched, falling onto the stomach

Note: The split axial in chapter 3, plate 22b, is an example of a lower lumbar arch. The stable position is enhanced by a pelvic tilt forward that allows the legs to split at maximum distance. The swimmer often errs by hyperextending the head, causing the position to become unstable (the presence of excessive traveling due to loss of balance).

When the swimmer has learned where to carry the head during transitions, and when to change its position to complement the timing of the movement from transition to stable position, many problems in figure execution will be eliminated.

A general guide for head positions in transitions:

1. The dolphin-type descent is enhanced by the head and shoulders pressing downward and backward as one unit.

2. The transition from front layout to the front pike position is most accurately performed when the head and chest press forward and downward as one unit.

3. While maintaining a ballet leg, as the torso passes through an arc or pivot from horizontal to near vertical, the head is held slightly forward with the chin pressed toward the neck. Example: slight flexion in the catalina, crane, etc. This same forward head position is used in back tuck somersaults or portions thereof; however, a greater degree of flexion is used.

4. Beginning in a front layout, when movement is toward the feet, with one leg passing through an airborne arc, the head is carried on the back of the shoulders.

5. When "walking out" of a figure by moving a leg toward the back through an airborne arc, the head and shoulders strongly press toward the water surface (thoracic arch). As the body surfaces, the back is straightened one vertebra at a time (or nearly so) and the head slowly returns to the plumb line.

Positioning the Shoulders

Body lines and balance are subject to the placement of the shoulders. The teacher-coach should sensitize the swimmer to the correct shoulder alignment, which involves the shoulder girdle. During horizontal layouts with the arms at the sides, the shoulders are held slightly retracted. Whereas, when vertical, the shoulders are slightly protracted. Although these positions are minute and represent an insignificant measurement on the screen of the Vanguard projector (one capable of reading angles), nevertheless, the swimmer can feel the position, and when they are present the line of the stable position is improved.

The shoulder position must not be overtaut. Tight shoulders inhibit the fluidity of the arm action because the upper arm and the shoulder girdle move together, providing additional range of motion in the shoulder joint. When the arm is abducted, the scapula rotates in the lateral plane of the body. Outward rotation of the upper arm is accompanied by retraction of the scapula in the shoulder girdle, while protraction accompanies inward rotation of the upper arm. From this brief description of complementary actions of the shoulder girdle and upper arm, the necessity for nontense shoulders to allow for the proper arm action is apparent.

Use of the Abdominals

Correct use of the abdominals will enable the swimmer to control two vital areas of the torso: the rib cage and the pelvis (cervical and lumbar). When horizontal or vertical, the upper abdominals should be strong enough to hold the base of the rib cage in line with the top of the hip bones. The lower abdominals must assist in holding the pelvis in line during leg action. Stability of the pelvis is also the result of a counterbalancing of the lower-back extensors with lower abdominals. The teacher-coach must observe the pelvis alignment, especially during the free movement of the legs about the hip joint. Those abdominal muscles controlling the pelvis must be strong enough to provide stability under the stress of the moving weight of the airborne legs.

Lack of abdominal strength will result in the pelvis tipping like a teeter-totter in the direction of the weight of the airborne legs. When the pelvis is correctly positioned (top of the hip bone plumb with shoulder), usually the thighs will appear correctly extended. However, a slight pelvic tilt is often the cause of many piked verticals and/or poor spinal alignment. There are three positions in which the pelvis may be carried: the mid position is used in verticals (a); a slight tilt toward the back is used in thrusting transitions (b); and the forward tilt is used in axial positions in which the back is arched (c).

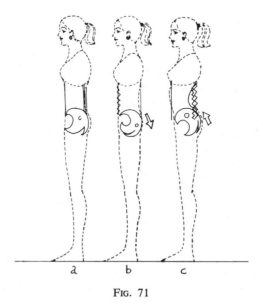

FIG. 71

We have said that the head was the key component in the anatomy of the figure. The position of the pelvis is also primary in the control of the fixed point around which other parts of the body move or are held static. For example, when tucking the body for a somersault, complete flexion of the spine necessitates tilting the pelvis backward (as shown in figure b), whereas complete hyperextension of the spine (arch), as used in the swordfish transition, necessitates tilting the pelvis forward (as shown in figure c). During vertical positions, in which the pelvis is slightly tilted backward (as in figure b), the thighs should appear completely extended. During axial positions in which the pelvis is tilted forward (as in figure c), the thighs should appear hyperextended at the hip joint. In great measure, the pelvic position should augment the position of the thighs and the remainder of the torso. The swimmer must learn these pelvic positions and relate each to the vertical and axial groups of figures.

Muscle Tone and Strength

The synchronized swimmer needs to be reminded to stretch the body full length in the water. Extension is perhaps the most important skill related to the figure design; it reveals the tone of the muscles in terms of strength and elasticity. Extension is readily observed in the legs (hip and knee joints), ankles, and insteps; the toes are plantar flexed.

Muscle strength must be coodinated with balance of the figure design. Balance is the result of muscle tension working as guy wires on all sides of the frame. Therefore, coaching the figure design involves telling the swimmer which groups of muscles to stretch and which to tighten to hold the skeletal frame in the desired position.

Use of Constant Speed

The swimmer must learn to use a constant speed during the transitional movements in figure performance. It is helpful to the swimmer if the coach counts during practice of schooled figures. A slow "and one and two" may be used for each transition until strength and endurance are increased. Progress to a slow count of "and one and two and three and four." Use a stop watch to determine the speed of the count. A guide to work toward is the use of four seconds for each transitional movement from one stable position to another. The time guide on page 187 for various figures was developed by the authors from their timing of over a hundred outstanding competitors at the United States national championships, and represents the mean times for each component or part thereof.

Elevation

Elevation is desirable in stable positions, unless otherwise described. It is also desirable in many transitional movements. In figure performance, *elevation* refers to the amount of body surface above the water line; it is used interchange-

TEMPO CHART

Figure Performed	Time (in seconds) Used to Execute
Ballet leg, single	16
Kip	12
Flamingo	24
Eiffel tower	28
Walkover, front	16
Dolphin	16
Barracuda, back pike	16
Hightower	22
Full twist from vertical	12
Vertical, forward split, twisting 180 degrees	8

Transition from ballet legs, double
    to vertical,
    as in the Flamingo
	4

ably with the word *height*. Elevation is aided by buoyancy, support sculling, and muscular uplift of the pelvic girdle. It may also be the result of propulsion. Elevation appears in figure performance in two distinctly different forms: *maximum height* and *maximum sustained height*.

Maximum height is the result of an effort to elevate the body by means of propulsion (scooping, sculling, feather press, hip lift, or shoulder press of the upper torso). It is an effort to reach the summit by exerting a force that is greater than gravity and strong enough to thrust or drive the body airborne. It is readily identified in thrusting figures and those transitions in which a strong scoop propels the body feet-first—Swordfish and Hightower, for example. Maximum height is not sustained. It is present momentarily in figure performance and is usually immediately followed by maximum sustained height.

Maximum sustained height, which is identified as controlled elevation of the body, is sustained by support sculling and represented by an unchanging water line. Maximum sustained height is an intergal part of figure transitions in which the legs are airborne, either motionless or in motion. It is also present when the torso is moving about the hips while passing from horizontal to vertical or vertical to horizontal. The key to sustained elevation during these transitions is strong support sculling and the use of a well-timed catch on the water as the body is eased from one stable position to another. A poorly timed catch will cause the hands to momentarily lose their anchoring hold on the water, the result of which will cause the water line to change. (The catch was described in chapter 4.) Maximum sustained height of the vertical high water line is the result of sculling at the lateral body line in the mid depth position. Such placement of the hands and arms assists stability of the vertical and will support the weight of the legs.

Effortlessness

Without effortlessness, movement in the water cannot be described as excellent synchronized swimming technique. When the swimmer is able to stretch, not strain, her body for proper alignment of the stable positions and slowly move from one stable position to another by stretching, effortlessness is enhanced. The effortless performance is smooth, having constant speed of action between stable positions; there is a mastery of muscle control and strength that reveals the swimmer's great ability to isolate movement. Without question, the effortless swimmer displays a unique capability and specialization in using the arms for support of weight or for propelling the body through the water. In addition, she makes maximum use of learning. The excellent competitive figure performer is the effortless swimmer who truly moves in and through the water as a graceful bird moves in and through the air.

COACHING THE ROUTINE

The coach directs the swimmer throughout the scheduled routine practices. She adds the finishing details to the performance. She is as familiar with the music as the choreographer; in fact, many times she is the choreographer. She demands good execution of all movements, never neglecting the seemingly less important parts—those that pass somewhat unnoticed. She appreciates that care for details characterizes all great aquatic performances. Often the coach extends her area of responsibility to selecting a light-weight costume for the team, one that will not impair execution. The student director in a high school or college assumes somewhat the same workload. To assist in recognizing the role of the coach of a routine, the following tips are offered. All are considered important.

Practicing the Routine

To perfect the component parts of the routine, the part-to-whole method is most effective. The pool practice time is divided and used for development of the routine figures and originals, the swimming of the routine strokes and variations, and for swimming the routine laps. The music is introduced following coach approval of the swimmers' execution of the skills incorporated in the routine. A variable-speed record player will be needed. At first, the music tempo may be slowed until all swimmers are familiar with the choreography and until they are able to identify the musical phrases with corresponding movement. Deck practice with the music at normal speed may be held at the pool site, or in a room, under the direction of the coach or student director. Deck practice contributes primarily to learning the movement sequences, becoming familiar with the tempo, and memorizing the musical score. To aid the swimmer in learning the routine, it is helpful to identify the movements that mark the beginning and the ending of each lap of the pool. Each swimmer should make a written copy of the routine, describing the movements in proper sequence for each lap (competitive routines lap the pool three to four times). Every swimmer of a routine needs a copy of the music. Cassette recordings are ideal.

Refinement of Routine Parts

The coach directs her attention toward refinement of routine parts until the execution of those parts is nearly flawless or commensurate with the skill of the swimmers. Those areas within the routine that are under constant scrutiny and are given constructive criticism are the use of strong flowing action, perfection in the execution of the figures and other transitions, the balance of space between swimmers, the establishment of the intended lines, the acute and precise timing of all movements with the music and with each swimmer, the projection of confidence and poise, the perfection of the deck dance, and the entrance into the water. The refinement of these parts cannot be achieved unless each swimmer is made aware of her performance faults. Therefore, each practice must be performed under the watchful eyes of the coach. A mental record of the observed errors is a gargantuan task. To assist the coach in recording the faults, we suggest the use of one of three practical methods:

a.   Record all errors as they occur on a transistor tape recorder. A recorder enables the coach to walk around the pool during the action. Several vantage points from which to view the swimmers are desirable because competitive routines are judged from the ends and the sides of the pool. During rest periods, the tape may be played back and corrections readily given.

b.   Use other swimmers on deck as spotters. Assign one member on deck to one in the water. Each spotter gives corrections to the swimmer at the conclusion of the routine performance.

c.   When coaching the routine without a tape recorder or extra spotters, use a prepared chart and one student assistant. The chart should provide a left column for the name of the swimmer and numerous columns to the right, indicating the most common faults. Examples: incorrect execution of figures, strokes, or variations; lacks endurance; forgets routine sequences; follows swimmers instead of music; lacks desired expression; poor spacing, poor timing of movement; cannot peak her performance more than once each practice session.

When the coach is fortunate enough to have other expensive equipment at her disposal, we suggest the use of video tapes or filming of the routine for a later showing. Film projected in slow motion reveals many details that otherwise are passed unnoticed.

The Solo

Coaching the soloist requires refinement of the most minute movement so that even the flick of the fingers adds to the performance. From the deck dance through to the climactic ending pose, the soloist must be strong yet not project labored strength in her control of movements. She should have an appealing style and a vast repertoire of skills. Often the soloist benefits from the assistance of a dance instructor to help with arm movements, design in space, development of expression, grace, and smoothness.

The Duet

Coaching the duet involves creating a carbon copy. Because the challenge is to look alike, duet partners should be of the same skill level. Each swimmer must be synchronized with a partner and with the music. Partners should feel and express movement in the same manner; whether the dynamics are bold and crisp or subdued and smooth, duet partners must be capable of expressing with identical form.

Spacing is important to successful surface patterns. Closed spacing is slightly more than an arm's length; open spacing is the width of a racing lane. Usually duets use closed spacing. Good spacing that does not weave is achieved by the use of visual markers along the pool wall or deck. It is not to be accomplished by watching a partner. Numerals along the sides of the pool, the black lines, the diving board, a clock or ladder should be used to guide the swimmers.

The Team

The problems of variation among swimmers are multipled when coaching the team routine. Inexperienced team members need leaders who understand spacing, underwater changes, and the distance to cover in one or more stroke patterns. Therefore, it is wise to keep a nucleus of experienced swimmers on the team.

Surface patterns should be varied and readily recognized in team routines. Swimmers must move about on the water surface to form either symmetrical or asymmetrical designs; they must also move under water to strategic positions before returning to the surface. Good surface patterns are born out of good underwater positions. Team members must understand that the underwater recoveries and position changes are to be executed alike and in the same relative time frame. Inability to gauge the speed of the underwater action causes intermittent "popping up," as well as a loss in the intended surface pattern.

To aid the synchronization of all movements, it is recommended that each swimmer have a copy of the music, supplemented with a written analysis of the choreography. The written form should include the number of downbeats used for stable positions, transitional movements, strokes, recoveries, and position changes. As mentioned in this chapter, this data must be grouped according to the laps of the pool.

CONDITIONING

In this text, *conditioning* refers to the physical and mental preparedness for the demands of synchronized swimming. It means the body and mind are well nourished and rested. Sufficient muscular strength and emotional control are to be present in the swimmer to meet the demands of figure and routine performance.

There is a tendency to think of conditioning and training as synonymous. In a sense they are, because of the close interrelationship between them. For example, when a swimmer has been strengthened through aquatic exercises, carefully taught the techniques of a figure, and has practiced that figure incessantly, the coach may expect the swimmer to perform the sequence consistently well. However, if the swimmer is nervous and worried about her competitive chances, has been up late the night before the meet, and has filled her stomach with soft drinks, she has impaired her condition to perform.

High-level Performance

The synchronized swimmer, like all athletes, must develop the ability to perform at a high level and not display psychological or physiological fatigue. Such capacity is the result of both good training and conditioning programs. Frequent practice, coupled with good conditioning discipline, increases the rate of swimmer progress to an amazing speed of accomplishment. This ability is evidenced in the competitive clubs along the west coast of the United States where high-level performance is born out of quality training and conditioning sessions scheduled five to six times a week (approximately eighteen to twenty hours). In other parts of the United States where good training techniques and conditioning are present, however, progress has been comparatively slow because the training is not frequent enough. Practicing twice a week (approximately four hours) is insufficient. Moreover, practice without emphasis on conditioning, and with little time spent on training methods as outlined, will produce swimmers with a tendency to execute in what the AAU synchronized swimming handbook calls the unsatisfactory class of performance.

Clubs that produce quality performance are dedicated to development of the physical skills of each swimmer. These are the clubs that undoubtedly will produce the first U. S. olympic team.

Synchronized swimmers who are sincere about their development as competitors lose interest when improvement is slight. We suggest, therefore, that the training methods used in speed swimming be adapted to the needs and specificity of the competitive synchronized swimmer to ensure the development of strength and endurance. Deck warm-up exercises should be designed to aid flexibility of the joints, including the spine. Isolated movements of body parts (the head, shoulders, pelvis, and legs) should be repeated to insure correct positioning of these parts to produce harmony between line and balance. Deck exercises must also include stretching and isotonic movements for the building of strength, especially in the arms. Refer to chapter 6, "Developmental Exercises for the Synchronized Swimmer."

Developing Strength and Endurance

We said in chapter 2 that sculling races and efficiency sculling tests should be used to strengthen the novice competitor. Such races should be conducted in the form of relays in which interval training is applied (repeats after controlled rest periods).

Weight in the form of single or double ballet legs may be added to sculling races as a kind of isotonic exercise to develop strength and endurance.

Modified long-distance stroke races are excellent for pacing the synchronized swimmer for routine performance. We previously suggested the swimming of at least twenty lengths of the pool to music as a warm-up exercise. Such conditioning improves the swimmers' abilities to perform at top capacity for four or five minutes, the length of the swimming routine.

The interval training method is applicable to the practice of the egg beater kick. Such practice benefits cardiorespiratory conditioning and strengthens the legs, both of which are necessary when swimming the routine.

Improvement of Neuromuscular Control

Stable positions, listed in chapter 3, and figure transitions, listed in chapter 5, should be included in each pool session. Just as the diving coach selects the dives, the coach should select, prior to the class, the three or four positions and transitions to be practiced. Each should be repeated six to eight times. The coach must encourage the swimmer to think about controlling buoyancy, weight, and gravity while practicing the stable positions, whereas, during the practice of figure transitions, the swimmer must concentrate on relaxing and stretching the joint that is to be moved slowly and effortlessly (Eutonie method).[3]

Sculling in the relative plane, scooping, and pulling are strengthened, and timing is perfected as stable positions and transitions are repeated. These arm movements must be as near to an involuntary reflex as habit will permit. The mind should be free to allow the swimmer full concentration on the joint(s) to be moved during a transition.

[3] Margaret C. Brown and Betty K. Sommer, *Movement Education: Its Evolution and a Modern Approach* (Reading, Mass.: Addison-Wesley Publishing Company, 1969).

Other Conditioning Aids

Practice of underwater swimming increases the athletes' abilities to hold the breath while performing in figure competition, in which fatigue must be retarded under conditions of slowed respiration for periods of twenty to thirty seconds.

We suggest that figure performers wet down before they perform in the figure event. Often the water is too cold (below eighty-two degrees Fahrenheit) for the slow muscle action used in figure performance. Wetting down helps psychological and physiological adjustments to whatever the temperature may be.

Conditioning includes good eating and sleeping habits. Foods high in protein values are recommended; soft drinks, fried foods, alcoholic beverages, tobacco, and drugs must be restricted. Swimmers should feel rested before they compete or practice.

The synchronized swimmer is hampered by overweight. Height on figures can be impaired by excessive weight around the hip and thighs. Overweight often causes laborious joint action, and energy is wasted overcoming buoyancy caused by fatty tissues. We recommend the overweight competitive synchronized swimmer seek professional guidance in weight-losing diets.

SUMMARY

1. The coach, who is responsible for the growth of synchronized swimming,
    a. structures the program,
    b. determines methods for developing the swimmer,
    c. motivates the swimmer,
    d. sets goals,
    e. directs the water show,
    f. conducts clinics, meets, and demonstrations, and
    g. trains officials.
2. Synchronized swimming was first called water ballet and is now a competitive sport.
3. Competitive synchronized swimming classes include stroking to music, development of figures, practice of routines, and conditioning methods.
4. Coaching aids include loop films, demonstrations by expert figure and stroke performers, and the use of a jointed cardboard mannequin.
5. Developmental exercises are prescribed for individual performance problems.
6. The position of the head is the key component in figure execution.
7. Figure design is taught by the part-to-whole method: alignment of body parts and muscular action.

8. Constant speed during transitional movement is desirable.

9. Elevation of the fixed point is desirable in figure performance.

10. Effortless action is associated with excellent performance.

11. When rehearsing the routine, organize the practice time for development of routine figures and originals, swimming the routine strokes, and swimming the routine laps.

12. Special emphasis is given to routine parts: the use of strong flowing action, perfection in figures and transitions, balance of space between swimmers, establishment of lines, synchronization with music and with other swimmers, projection of confidence and poise, precision in the deck movement, and the entry into the water.

13. Recording performance faults may be accomplished by the use of a tape recorder, a spotter, or a check list.

14. The soloist must be strong but effortless in her movements, show great variety of skills, and have an appealing style in her performance.

15. Duet partners must look alike in their performance techniques, use the same dynamics in movements, keep lines well spaced, and be of the same skill level.

16. The team routine requires perfection in surface patterns, underwater recoveries, synchronization, and figure execution.

17. Conditioning and training refer to the physical and mental preparedness for the demands of the sport.

18. Conditioning and training include interval training in which the activity is repeated after controlled rest periods; adding weight to sculling for developing strength and endurance; and swimming long-distance races to prepare for the swimming of the routine.

19. In figure performance, improvement of neuromuscular control is developed through practice of transitions while concentrating on the joint to be moved by stretching slowly and effortlessly.

20. Other conditioning aids include underwater swimming, wetting down before the schooled figure event, eating high-protein foods, regulating body weight, refraining from using alcoholic beverages, tobacco, drugs, and soft drinks, and getting rest before competition or practice.

8

THE ROUTINE
CHOREOGRAPHY

Today's competitive routines reflect the depth of experience accumulated in a full quarter of a century. The choreographer knows how to combine aquatic movements so that the final composition is outstanding stylistically from both a dance and sports viewpoint. Movements that tended to be awkward in the water have been replaced with artistic actions that both make use of the water and are scientifically possible to perform. The dance media has not only contributed greatly to authentic arm movements but has also assisted in the development of creative choreography appropriate for the water. Although the routine is written primarily to reflect the swimmers' skills, the choreographer is also cognizant of audience response and its role in competition. When the routine is well written and well performed, the choreographer expects at least three moments of audience spontaneity during the performance. This response may be a hand clap for perfection of either a simple or difficult maneuver, an emotional response (joy, sadness, love, hate), or a moment when the crowd identifies greatness through a spine-tingling spirit emitted by the performers.

Experience has taught the choreographer to work closely with the swimmers. It is considered wise to allow the swimmers opportunity to evaluate the actions within the routine and to recreate sections when necessary. When all members concerned with the routine have approved and accepted the choreography, the spirit to proceed and to perform have been strengthened.

RULES CONTROLLING THE ROUTINE

Competitive routines are written primarily to fit the skills of the athlete and must comply with the rules of the governing organization. The routine skeleton written for AAU competition is somewhat predetermined in that five required schooled figures from at least three different categories must be included in the composition. However, the Midwest Intercollegiate synchronized swimming rules covering the routine closely parallel those of the Federation of International Athletics in that the routine is a "free" aquatic exercise with no required schooled figures. A free routine is also permitted in the festivals conducted by the Academy of Aquatic Art. In routine competition we foresee the complete gamut of competitive opportunity opening to the high school girl in interscholastic meets; the college student through intercollegiate meets; and a potpourri of swimmers in the AAU swimming programs. Because the rules in each governing organization vary in application to the swimming routine, the choreographer should be conversant with all rules of the sport.

GENERAL CONSTRUCTION OF THE ROUTINE

The choreographer must be sensitive to the limitations as well as to the freedom of creativity in an aquatic environment. Original ideas must be designed to work in the water, where resistance is greater than on the stage and where the very nature of the water removes the stability to which the performers are accustomed when on firm ground. Consideration must be given to the limited amount of air space available to the swimmer for designs in space (the length of the arms or legs when above the water surface). The swimmer cannot jump, run, or even walk in deep water. With all these limitations there yet remains a challenging array of the possible. It is with this thought in mind that the choreographer takes up the elements of dance and combines them with the techniques and skills of synchronized swimming to create the spectacular swimming routine.

Guided by the rhythmical structure of the music, the skill of the swimmer, and the purpose for the routine, the movements are created and timed to fit each phrase in the musical score. For competition or for entertaining the water show audience, good aquatic compositions should be constructed so that each phrase has a recognizable "shape," with a beginning, a body, and an ending. The phrases are tied together with surface transitions that add continuity to the movement and complement the flow of action. A disjointed collection of aquatic skills should be avoided. Stroking is used when the music suggests traveling; figures and originals, when the rhythm is accentuated; and floats, when the melody is soft and devoid of percussive instruments. These are the three basic ingredients of the routine. However, a fourth ingredient—the use of the arms in airborne designs—has been increasingly effective throughout the routine, culminating in a coda (a passage of music and movement that concludes the routine). Music from the classics, semiclassics, ballet, theatrical musicals, and quality pops should be used for the competitive routine. Contrary to the free exercise in gymnastics, in which a solo instrument accompanies the gymnast, the synchronized routine at its best is accompanied by a symphony orchestra.

ELEMENTS OF COMPOSITION

Following selection of the music and general theme, the choreographer needs creative water sessions with the swimmers. During these sessions, original figures, floats, and kaleidoscopic patterns are created. Also, the choreographer becomes acquainted with the skills of the swimmers. The ideas from these water sessions are incorporated into a routine that complies with examples of the principles of good composition: sequence, balance, transition, contrast, variation, harmony, repetition, and climax. These elements represent the *form* factors of the routine. Together, all factors must aim toward unity of the whole.

The person who truly calls herself a choreographer of synchronized swimming must possess an in-depth understanding of the space and rhythmic factors inherent to the dance routine. Because these factors have long been an integral part of the dance and are desirable for swimming routines, we suggest the use and unique blending of these elements in the aquatic composition. The chart on the following page represents and integrates all the elements of dance routines and applies also to the needs of the choreographer of the swimming routines.

When the choreographer is highly skilled and experienced, it is possible to draft the routine on paper. Only minor adjustments may be needed once the routine is taken to the water. More often, however, it is advisable to try the movement phrases in the water to substantiate the "swimability" of each.

Because the choreography is judged in two distinctly different categories— the *techniques of execution* and the *content*—it is an advantage for the choreographer to work with the coach during the period of composing and while the swimmers are learning the routine. Quite frequently the choreographer has a greater talent to offer in development of the routine content, whereas the coach is an expert on techniques used in execution. When the composer is satisfied with the construction of the routine and has conveyed the intended interpretation of the elements, her responsibility to the routine ends.

SUMMARY

1. Aquatic compositions are constructed so that each phrase has a shape: a beginning, a body, and an ending.
2. Swimmers of competitive routines have three national outlets for competing: the Midwest Intercollegiate Synchronized Swimming Organization, the Academy of Aquatic Art, and the AAU.
3. The choreographer's tools for phrasing the routine are listed in chart III, "The Woven Fabric."

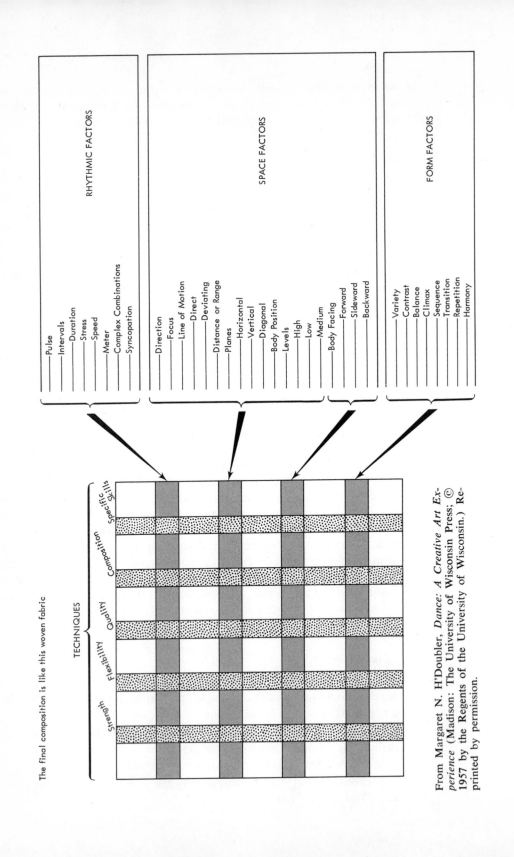

The final composition is like this woven fabric

RHYTHMIC FACTORS

Pulse
Intervals
Duration
Stress
Speed
Meter
Complex Combinations
Syncopation

SPACE FACTORS

Direction
Focus
Line of Motion
Direct
Deviating
Distance or Range
Planes
Horizontal
Vertical
Diagonal
Body Position
Levels
High
Low
Medium
Body Facing
Forward
Sideward
Backward

FORM FACTORS

Variety
Contrast
Balance
Climax
Sequence
Transition
Repetition
Harmony

TECHNIQUES

Strength
Flexibility
Quality
Composition
Specific Skills

From Margaret N. H'Doubler, *Dance: A Creative Art Experience* (Madison: The University of Wisconsin Press; © 1957 by the Regents of the University of Wisconsin.) Reprinted by permission.

9

JUDGING COMPETITIVE
SYNCHRONIZED SWIMMING

In the world of amateur sports, thousands of girls and women are participating in competitive synchronized swimming. The schooled figure event, comparable to the *required figure* event in competitive ice skating, is an integral part of the total competition and is followed by the swimming routine, which is comparable to the *skating routine*. The swimming competition also has parallels with gymnastics. The gymnast performs *sequences on the apparatus* for a panel of judges; similarly, the synchronized swimmer executes figures in the water. Both the gymnast's *free exercise* and the synchronized swimmer's routine are performed to music and judged by a panel of experts.

A competitive sport that depends on a panel of judges to determine the winner and runners-up must provide a training program that is accessible to persons from all parts of the country and the world. The national judges' rating and training committee for the AAU and a similar committee for DGWS (Division of Girls' and Women's Sports) offer training and testing programs. Basically, the training consists of a study of the AAU *Handbook for Synchronized Swimming:* a written, a practical, and an oral examination. These organizations conduct training clinics for the potential judge where experts are heard, films of championships are shown, and live demonstrations of schooled figures are presented.

It is often said that a competitive synchronized swimming coach is best prepared to judge the schooled figures and routine events. We feel this is true because the coach is completely familiar with stable positions, transitional movement, and the elements within a routine. Generally, the competitive coach justifiably claims an in-depth understanding of schooled figures and stroke techniques. However, when judging, a coach who is closely associated with a competitor may unintentionally favor or disfavor that competitor.

IDENTIFICATION OF PRIMARY JUDGING ELEMENTS

Similar to diving, the figure performance passes before the eye of the judge within a few seconds, whereas the swimming routine is constant action for four to five minutes. In each event, the judge is required to quickly recognize and evaluate the *primary elements* present in the performance and judge the composite of these elements against the best known performance (from the standpoint of perfection). To maintain an up-to-date image of perfection, the judge must attend top-level national competition. When this is not possible, films of the champions should be reviewed and studied. Loop films of schooled figures are available for rent or purchase at the Jole Company, P.O. Box 6034, San Jose, California. Films of current routines must be secured through AAU synchronized swimming clubs or private individuals.

In judging AAU schooled figures, two major elements are evaluated: design and control. The *design* of the figure refers to its *line* or lines, and its maximum value is five points. The line is readily observed and its accuracy measured according to vertical, horizontal, or axial in relation to the water surface.

The *control* of a figure includes elevation (height), extension, compactness, constant tempo, timing, effortlessness, and a performance that is relatively stationary. Its maximum value is five points. The degree of perfection within the design and the control is represented in one composite score, from zero to ten points.

In judging an AAU swimming routine, two major aspects are evaluated: *execution* and *content*. Each is scored separately from the other on a scale from zero to ten with tenths of points beginning with five tenths. Execution covers the strokes, schooled figures and parts thereof as well as other propulsion techniques. These are judged from a standpoint of perfection.

Content is composed of several components: synchronization, creative action fluidity, difficulty, and diversity. Each of these components has been assigned a numerical value representing its relationship to a total of ten points. The composite content score reflects the degree of perfection of all these components.

When judging the performance of a figure or a routine, the degree of perfection is commensurate with one of six evaluative categories: failed, deficient, unsatisfactory, satisfactory, good, and excellent. A range of scores that has been assigned to each category appears later in this chapter.

This chapter was written to assist the prospective judge; the information presented is basic for all who serve the sport in an official capacity. The following material focuses first on the primary judging elements of the figure performance and then on those of the swimming routine.

To prepare for judging the figures, four basic steps are recommended:

1. The judge must learn the combined sequences that represent competitive schooled figures. The difficulty of each figure should be common knowledge.
2. The judge must know the primary elements to look for and to evaluate.
3. The judge must develop an understanding of the evaluative categories of performance and know the range of scores within each.
4. The judge must observe all levels of live performances, study movie films of swimmers of various skill levels, and attend local, regional, and national clinics.

These four areas of training are considered prerequisites for judging synchronized swimming. To prepare for a judges' rating test, we suggest a study of the schooled figure sequences in the AAU handbook, supplemented with chapters 3, 5, and 9 of this text.

IDENTIFICATION OF FIGURE DESIGN

Line   Value: 5 points

The analyses that follow describe the best performance today. As stated, line is the only element of design. The judging of the figure begins when the referee blows the whistle or gives the command "Go." All figures begin in either the front or back layout position. Judging the body line of each stable position in relation to the water surface merits first priority.

HORIZONTAL LINE (FRONT AND BACK LAYOUT)

The horizontal line is referred to as the *gravity buoyancy line,* and in this text is abbreviated Gb. This line passes laterally along the body from head to toe. The proper horizontal body alignment is readily observed by the judge in that the water surface is synonymous with this line. For example, when in the back layout, the water surface passes through the following anatomical markings of the body: it begins at the top of the head above the ear, touches the cheek bone, a front portion of the shoulder, passes mid bust, the front of the hip bone, bisects the thigh, passes through the ankle, and terminates at the little toe.

The front layout position has a Gb line that begins at the top of the head, passes behind the ear (head in the water), exposes a small portion of the shoulders, bisects the buttocks and thigh, exposes the heel, and terminates in the little toe. To attain this line, swimmers must neither hyperextend the back nor stretch the abdominals. When the head and face are held above the water (optional position), the remainder of the body should not deviate from the line described. Those swimmers who are less buoyant will be required to scull more rapidly to produce enough uplift to comply with the line.

BALLET LEG LINE

The delineation of the stable positions in which a leg or legs are held airborne imposes the assessment of two lines, the vertical *plumb line,* referred to as Pl, and Gb line. The Pl line extends through anatomical markings of the airborne leg, creating a line perpendicular to the water surface. For example, the Pl line of a single or double ballet leg position is a lateral line that passes outside the little toe, runs through the ankle, a point outside the knee joint, and terminates in the hip. This line represents the correct placement of the leg to the water surface, not to the upper torso. During the holding of the single ballet leg, the horizontal Gb line of the body is altered from that previously described in the back layout. This line passes from the top of the head, through the cheek bone, and exposes the instep and the toes of the horizontal leg. The hips and the horizontal thigh are not expected to touch the Gb line. However, support and body extension should be strong enough to hold the hips near the water surface so that the water line bisects the upper thigh of the ballet leg. The double ballet legs position has a Gb line that passes through the top of the head, cheek bone, and above the knee. Excellent height in the double ballet legs position reveals a water line at mid thigh. The Pl line is identical to the single ballet leg position (ninety degrees to the water surface).

VERTICAL LINES

When the body is vertical and supported at near ankle depth, the vertical Pl line is slightly to the front of the lateral body line. It touches the little toe, ankle bone, front of the knee joint, the hip, shoulder, cheek bone, and top of the head. The balanced vertical does not travel in the water when all the anatomical markings are in line. The body will gain height above the water with minimal sculling until the airborne weight is equal to the uplifting force. No muscular strain is apparent except for that which is required to hold the head and torso in good posture, the legs and ankles extended, and the toes plantar flexed.

The forward split vertical (crane-fishtail) has a vertical Pl line comparable to the vertical low water line as previously described. The horizontal Gb line passes through the horizontal leg. When this position is stabilized at its maximum sustained height, the water line will cross the upper one third of the vertical thigh, and pass through the ankle of the horizontal leg (the horizontal leg is not truly horizontal but slightly diagonal to the water surface).

The vertical variant (heron) has a vertical Pl line comparable to the forward split vertical. The line is slightly to the front of the body.

The front pike vertical has a horizontal Gb line that passes through the legs and hips, as described in the front layout. The Pl line is under water and perpendicular to the water surface as it passes laterally through the torso. The Pl line contacts the Gb line at the hips, creating a nintey-degree angle. The back is flattened so that the spinal line appears straight.

SUBMARINE LINE

Both the single ballet leg submarine and the double ballet legs submarine require the same anatomical alignment of the legs in relation to the water surface as described above. The significant difference is found in the torso line. In the submarine positions, the swimmer attempts to create a ninety-degree angle at the hips and at the water surface. This angle is present between the vertical leg and the torso, the vertical leg to the horizontal leg, and the vertical leg to the water surface.

AXIAL LINE

The back tuck closed position is compact but not overtaut. The thighs have been drawn to the chest, the back has been flexed, and the pelvis tilted backward to aid the lift of the hips to the water surface. The head has been flexed until the water line touches the eyebrows, approximately. Caution: the head should not be flexed to its maximum in an effort to compensate for the inability to flex the total spine. The back tuck closed position is a stress position in which the muscles must be conditioned to hold. The Gb line is synonymous with the water surface. It passes through the little toe, the ankle bone, and laterally along the lower leg. A small portion of the buttocks is exposed. The water line touches the eyebrows. When this position is tipped backward one quarter (approximately), it becomes the tuck axial. The Gb line exposes a small portion of the buttocks and bisects the lower legs between the knee and the heel.

The front tuck position represents the same placement of body parts as used in the back tuck. The water line passes through the flexed back, exposing a portion of the spine. The head is flexed and submerged.

The split axial is illustrated among twenty-five other stable positions in chapter 3. The upper torso and head are slightly arched and the pelvis is tilted forward to assist the horizontal leg at the back of the swimmer. The Gb line touches each ankle bone, exposing the instep and the toes of the arched leg, the heel, and ball of the foot of the flexed leg. The hips are held near the water surface by either mid-depth or bottom-depth sculling at the lateral line. The width of the split gives the illusion of the legs being nearly horizontal to the water.

The reverse split axial has a Pl line that passes along the little toe and ankle, and outside the knee, hip, shoulder, and cheek bone. The Gb line passses along the ankle bone of the horizontal leg to the back of the body (the lower back is arched).

The split axial variant position is one of complete arch. The Gb line exposes the instep of the horizontal leg to the back of the body and a portion of the flexed knee.

IDENTIFICATION OF FIGURE CONTROL

Primary Elements   **Composite value: 5 points**

The elements of control are so interwoven and interrelated to the stable positions and transitions that a fine mental sieve is needed to separate one from the other. Because these elements are present throughout the total figure and are not recognized in particular sequence, one may well expect only the most experienced judge to see and evaluate each element according to its degree of perfection. We hope the descriptions that follow will assist the judge in developing an image and an understanding for each element of control.

ELEVATION—MAXIMUM HEIGHT
AND MAXIMUM SUSTAINED HEIGHT

The dictionary defines maximum height as a climbing to or elevation to the summit. Maximum height is the result of a driving force that is greater than the force of gravity acting upon the body and strong enough to move the body weight airborne. As we have seen in chapter 7, maximum height is not sustained. Present momentarily, it is the result of propulsion, either primary (arms) or secondary (body press). When it is the result of primary propulsion, the arms drive the body airborne by propulsion sculling, scooping, or a combination referred to as a feather press. When it is the result of secondary propulsion, the elevation of the body is aided by a body press. Thrusting figures are an example. Maximum height resulting from a body press appears during transitions found in the heron and barracuda family of schooled figures, the spiral and the pivot roll used in the subalina. The body actually climbs airborne by means of secondary propulsion before it is stablized at its maximum sustained height.

Maximum sustained height, the result of support sculling, is constant. It has an unchanging water line during both the holding of stable positions and during the transitional movement of the legs. Maximum sustained height of the front and back layout positions is measured by the Gb line described earlier in this chapter. The same is true of the front tuck, back tuck, and the front pike positions. Maximum sustained height of the pelvic area of the body relative to the water surface is best understood after examining what has thus far been identified in performances given by the best competitors. During the holding and balance of a high water line vertical, the most excellent maximum sustained height of this position has a water line above the knees. The forward split vertical (crane) and the vertical variant (heron) positions have a maximum sustained height very near the hips. Maximum sustained height in the split axial reveals that if the swimmer is flexible through the back and hip joints, it is possible to maintain the base of the hips just slightly under the water surface. Unless the champion figure performers are allowed to use enlarged webbed hands, it is doubtful that greater sustained heights will be relatively stationary because of the laws of physics related to a body immersed in water.

EXTENSION AND COMPACTNESS

The degree of extension, hyperextension, or flexion is another judging element. The ability to stretch horizontally, vertically, or in a circular line is basic to the execution of schooled figures, as is the ability to make the body compact by flexion of its parts. In figure performance, extension is measured by the human eye according to the accuracy of the vertical Pl line and the horizontal Gb line in relation to the level water surface. Unlocked knees and the presence of an angle between the instep and the shin are evidences of underdeveloped extension of the levers of the legs. It is the responsibility of the judge to evaluate extension of the body parts above and below the water. When the body is in a back layout or vertical, a forward head and a tilted pelvis are weaknesses in the extension of the torso; axial positions, on the other hand, are best performed when the parts of the spine and the head are arranged so as to create a continuous curved line by means of hyperextension or flexion.

EFFORTLESSNESS

Effortlessness has been discussed in chapter 7. It is best described as a blending of strength and flexibility with learning. Identified with steady, smooth action devoid of strain, it is the result of muscle preparedness for the holding of stress positions. When effortless movement is performed, only those levers involved in the action should move. Movement should begin slowly, progress steadily through the distance required, then decrease in speed to allow the levers to ease to a stop. The ability to stretch with ease away from the mid-body line or contract toward the mid line enhances effortlessness. Synchronized swimming fosters a slender figure that claims strength to stretch away from the center-body line or place the body parts in a comparatively small ball. During airborne leg action, effortlessness is destroyed by a splash down of the legs on the water. Such a rapid deposit of weight causes poor balance, the recovery of which destroys effortlessness. Because balance in the water is a delicate position, the slightest change in distribution of body weight will cause muscle action of the torso and extraneous action of the arms. An attempt to save a position lacking in balance will destroy effortlessness.

RELATIVELY STATIONARY CONTROL

A relatively stationary schooled figure is best described as sequences of movement successively performed around a fixed point. Depending on the body position, the fixed point is located either within the pelvic area of the body or outside of the body. When the fixed point is within the body, support sculling is imperative during movement around that point. For example, during secondary propulsion, a shoulder press downward and backward around the fixed point, as in the flamingo figure, moves the torso to vertical. During this action, the arms and hands supply sculling uplift and support for the fixed point. As the torso nears vertical, a catch is executed at mid depth, followed by a lateral feather press, representing the essential support techniques that increase stability of the fixed point and enhance the vertical. In contrast, if during the torso descent the swimmer elects to use an arm pull to assist secondary propulsion, the mid-depth catch and the feather press must be excluded—there isn't time for both techniques before sinking below the surface. Inevitably the body will travel off its stationary point because the pull is primary propulsion in a headfirst direction. When it is used prematurely before vertical alignment, it will move the body downward and backward off its fixed point. With few exceptions, whenever the torso is pressed downward from horizontal to vertical, or vice versa, around a fixed point, support techniques produce a relatively stationary flow of action. Technically, as the torso moves downward, the fulcrum of the arm (shoulder joint) and the resistance arm (hand) are subsequently moved to a position of poor mechanical advantage. To control the concentration of weight at the fixed point, the swimmer must move the holding force (hands) to mid depth, where a greater purchase on the water is sufficient to support the weight. The fixed point is extremely vulnerable to the force of gravity when both airborne legs are centered approximately over this point.

Travel off the fixed point is frequently a problem for the swimmer while moving from the tuck axial tip up to vertical high water line (kip transition). Poor timing of the torso press with the lift of the legs causes movement of the fixed point.

During movement of a static body position in which propulsion is used, the fixed point is outside the body. The dolphin and back pike somersault are good examples. The fixed point of the dolphin is outside and below the beginning position of the body. The fixed point of the somersault is below the hips. Sculling propels the dolphin throughout, whereas scoops, pulls, and sculling propel the somersault. Such schooled figures are difficult to judge because of water refraction, the necessity for the swimmer to overcome inertia, and the imaginary placement of a fixed point.

A limited amount of forward momentum is acceptable in transitions that begin in a front layout and move downward headfirst to, or through, the front pike vertical. The amount of primary propulsion of the arms should be enough to overcome inertia and complement secondary propulsion. Best results are attained from using primary propulsion (arms) first followed by a chest press. When these two forces are blended, the illusion created may very well appear nearly stationary. The judge may readily identify unequal force between primary and secondary propulsion in the transition from a front layout through the pike somersault to the double ballet legs submarine position. The use of a strong chest press preceding primary propulsion will cause the hips to pop out of the water, immediately followed by the sinking of the pelvis and legs, whereas the use of strong primary propulsion unbalanced with a chest press will pull the hips and legs underwater while attempting to move from a front layout to the front pike vertical. In either case, the body is unable to move an equal distance around the fixed point because of a faulty propulsion sequence. A swimmer who has developed a blending of the two forces (primary and secondary) will successfully move the torso and legs along the outside of the geometric pattern describing the required design while remaining an equal distance from the fixed point. Finally to move the torso downward from a front layout position, primary propulsion is followed by secondary propulsion, enabling the body to remain an equal distance from the fixed point, amounting to relatively stationary action.

CONSTANT TEMPO

In the figure performance, the use of a slow constant tempo helps to eliminate the possibility of a strong adverse reaction of the water against the body. The concept of *for every action there is an equal and opposite reaction* dictates the use of slow, steady movement. The swimmer should always attempt to keep the resistance of the water within the range of maximum control with little effort. See the tempo chart in chapter 7 for a sample of the tempos used by several U. S. champions.

TIMING

Timing is as integral to the execution of the total figure as it is to a rendition by a symphony orchestra: unless all parts are perfectly cued, the performance disintegrates. The timing of a figure represents the moment when one movement begins and another is finished. To be well timed, the figure is executed so that all movements are coordinated, including the support and propulsion techniques. In general, the judge may associate good timing with good control in that the body muscles appear to respond with measured strength sufficient for the work-load. Poor timing is often the cause of imbalance, a partial loss of height, deviation from the prescribed line, and movement of the fixed point. Often poor timing produces a frantic attempt to save a performance by the use of unorthodox techniques.

The words *timing* and *tempo* are used interchangeably by mistake. A slow or rapid performance of a figure describes its tempo, not necessarily its timing.

When judging the elements of control in figure competition (as discussed previously), the elements are grouped together to determine their worth. When all the elements are excellent, a maximum of five points may be assigned to the figure control. When the elements are above satisfactory approximately 3.5 to four points are given. Average control is worth approximately 2.5 to three points, whereas unsatisfactory control is worth approximately 1.5 to two. Deficient control is worth approximately .5 to 1.5. The figure design element (line) is evaluated in the same manner and added to the value of the control to arrive at a final overall score for the schooled figure.

Following the study of this text, which has identified and discussed stable positions, transitional movement, support techniques, including the sculling depths, propulsion forms, and the primary elements of figure design and control, hopefully the judge will be as familiar with the total figure as the maestro is familiar with the symphonic rendition he directs.

When scoring the execution of AAU schooled figures, the performance is compared and evaluated according to the categorical descriptions that follow. An appropriate range of points has been assigned to each category. The total scale of points is from zero to ten with half-point gradations.

DESCRIPTION OF SCHOOLED FIGURE CATEGORIES

Failed   **Score: zero point**

A failed figure is a combination of one or more stable positions with one or more transitions executed in a sequence unrelated to a described competitive schooled figure, or one or more stable positions combined with one or more transitions that represent another described competitive schooled figure. A failed figure is one that is unrecognizable. This means there was an attempt to perform the figure but that half or more of the total number of sequences within the figure were not performed. (A single stable position combined with the prescribed single transition in proper order constitutes a sequence.) The omission of a sequence usually does not constitute a failed figure, but the figure is subject to a referee's penalty. In no way should the penalty affect the judge's score, however; the judge must always evaluate the design and control elements and select the category that best describes the total performance. The referee enforces the penalty.

Deficient   **Score: .5 to 2.5 points**

When the design and three or more primary elements of control are of poor quality, the performance is deficient. The figure, therefore, constitutes major potential deficiencies. For example, when the line is faulty in each stable position, with a considerable deviation from the Gb and Pl lines, and the water line is several inches below the maximum sustained height known for each stable position, the degree of perfection is deficient; or, when the toes are not flexed, the ankles not extended, and movement within the body levers is stiff, jerky, and laborious, so that the body travels off its fixed point, major deficiencies are present. A deficient performance usually has weak sculling. Often the support sculling is executed at an improper depth to complement the inaccuracy of the body alignment.

Unsatisfactory   **Score: 3 to 4.5 points**

One or two of the stable positions within the figure are not aligned; therefore, balance is not present throughout. Some traveling is in evidence and the water line fluctuates from the maximum sustained height to one of less height. However, movement is performed with greater ease than in the deficient category, showing an improvement of the primary control elements. Because the timing of the body presses and the arm patterns are not coordinated, an intermittent uplift of the fixed point is noticeable. Secondary propulsion (a body press) is too rapid and forceful, creating an imbalance between primary and secondary propulsion.

Satisfactory   **Score: 5 to 6.5 points**

The stable positions are in line and the body balanced, permitting the transitional movement to flow around a stationary point. Elevation is near the maximum sustained height for each stable position. The legs are stretched and firm at the hips during airborne action. Support sculling is coordinated with the change of body position, although it lacks smoothness and strength. Some transitions represent the blending of primary and secondary propulsion, although constant speed is not present throughout.

Good   **Score: 7.0 to 8.5 points**

All stable positions are in line. The levers of the body are stretched away from the joints during verticals, whereas during axials the spinal alignment is either flexed or hyperextended with ease. Transitional movement is graceful, slow, and consistently steady, enhanced by a noticeable degree of flexibility of the joints. Elevation is at the maximum sustained height for each stable position. Evidences of good training and conditioning of the body and mind produce an above-average degree of strength, proficiency, and confidence. Only the specific muscles needed to create the movement are involved in the actual movements, while others are stabilized. Both the agonistic and antagonistic muscles are conditioned to handle the shifting weight of the body. The performance is bathed in an array of graceful movement.

Excellent   **Score: 9 to 10 points**

All stable positions are aligned with ease, as if the water were holding the body. The body levers are slowly stretched and contracted. Movement is fluid. Support is strong, yet the speed of the sculling is relatively slow. The timing of the figure parts appears perfect. Maximum heights are attained by strong, slow, and fluid propulsion techniques.

To prepare for judging the routine, the following prerequisites are recommended:

1. Teaching advanced swimming
2. Class study in the fundamentals of synchronized swimming
3. Experience in choreography school or college water show routines
4. Experience as a student or teacher of modern dance, folk dance, or ballet
5. A year of apprenticeship training under a competitive synchronized swimming coach
6. A completion of the four basic steps recommended for judging figures (see beginning of this chapter)

The most respected judge of the routine event is the person who has completed the list of prerequisites. In addition, the judge who has exposure to national-caliber routines is sensitive to the degree of perfection that represents excellence. It is essential to establish a mental picture of excellence so that the best known performance may become the criterion against which all other performances are compared. Routines from any part of the United States or the world should be judged according to the same scale of standards. This is essential to stabilize judging and to establish a unified and consistent appraisal of the routine elements.

A retired competitor who has competed at various skill levels over several years has an excellent background for judging routines. The AAU, and DGWS seek out such individuals and encourage them to become judges. In this way, both organizations strengthen their judges' roster.

When judging an AAU synchronized swimming routine, two grades are awarded. One is for the execution of the figures, strokes, parts, and propulsion techniques. The second score is for the elements of content: synchronization, creative action, fluidity, difficulty, and diversity. All elements are judged from a standpoint of perfection. Tenths of points are used in the scoring of the routine, one-tenth of a point to ten points.

IDENTIFICATION OF PRIMARY ELEMENTS OF A ROUTINE

Execution   **Value: 10 points**

SCHOOLED FIGURES, ORIGINALS,
STROKES, AND PARTS

AAU routines are required to include five schooled figures of any difficulty from a list of competitive figures, which have been assigned to one of four groupings. No more than two figures from each group may be included in the total of five. Original figures are sequences created by the swimmer that may resemble competitive schooled figures and yet are unique in design. The judge need not discern between a required figure and an original figure; he must assess the execution of these movements according to the degree of proficiency based on the primary elements in the performance. There is, however, one exception. In routine performance, figures and originals do not necessarily start in a stationary position. During a ballet leg portion of a figure, the body may travel. Figures or originals that begin in a front layout usually are preceded by a stroke; therefore, for example, a greater distance is covered during the movement from front layout to the front pike vertical. An in-depth discussion of the judging of standard or hybrid strokes will not be included here. It is sufficient to say that the execution of strokes is evaluated according to the same primary elements listed under schooled figures. The execution score must represent the category that the figures, strokes, and parts best exemplify. Again, the categories are: excellent, good, satisfactory, unsatisfactory, deficient, and failed.

Content

SYNCHRONIZATION   *Value: 1.0 point solo; 4.0 points duet and team*

A judge who is endowed with a sense of rhythm and has trained in music and dance best fulfills the requirements for judging synchronization of movement with music, whereas no particular skills are needed to judge synchronization with a partner. The judge should be able to discern choreography that is synchronized with the rhythm of the music (counterpoint melodies or a singular melody); movement that is carefully executed, using the musical measures, phrases, transitional sections (codas), loud and soft parts, and staccato and legato (to determine its time, tempo, and interpretive qualities) is synchronized with the musical score. Partners are well synchronized when they swim strokes, execute figures, and perform all other parts simultaneously. In synchronization, all underwater and airborne movements are together; the surface of the water serves as a starting and finishing point for airborne action. When partners are totally synchronized with each other and with the music, they are inseparable.

CREATIVE ACTION   Value: 1.0 point solo; 1.0 point duet and team

Innovative surface patterns, moving floats, unique arm movements, and original figures contribute to creative action. Adaptations from dance (folk, modern, and ballet) enhance creativity. Experimentation with various body positions contributes to original designs in space and on the water surface. Also contrast in the speed of execution will enhance the swimmers' creativeness.

FLUIDITY   Value: 2.0 points solo; 1.0 point duet and team

Once the music begins, it flows along a rhythmical pattern. To best use the fluidity of the music, all movement must flow in some direction. Transitions that connect strokes to figures, or vice versa, and other propulsion techniques, such as sculling and kicking, aid fluidity. When all parts of the choreography (beginning, body, and ending) flow together, the action is considered fluid.

DIFFICULTY   Value: 4.0 points solo; 3.0 points duet and team

The scale of difficulty applicable to synchronized swimming figures is from 1.1 to 2.2. Since only competitive schooled figures have been assigned a difficulty, to help the judge discern the difficulty of component movements, such movements have been grouped in the following high to low difficulty guide.

HIGH TO LOW DIFFICULTY GUIDE

a. Those complex movements around a fixed point that begin with both legs airborne and progress while holding the water line near the hips are most difficult. A repeat of such movement in a series adds to the difficulty.

b. With few exceptions, those complex movements around a fixed point that begin with one leg airborne and progress while holding the water line near the hips are moderately difficult.

c. Movements described in a and b correspondingly decrease in difficulty when the water line is supported at mid calf.

d. Movements involving only secondary propulsion are least difficult, for example, log roll. Note: Standard or hybrid stroking is considered simple and less difficult than egg beater support of airborne arms. See component difficulty charts in the appendix.

DIVERSITY   Value: 1.0 point solo; 1.0 point duet and team

The judge assesses diversity of the choreography by noting the variety of skills incorporated in the routine. We have said that the competitive figures must be selected from at least three various groups; however, original figures, when diverse, should represent at least four of the following variety groupings:

a. The ballet leg
b. The somersault
c. The circle or part thereof
d. Combinations of the first three
e. Stroking, hybrid, or variations
f. Split verticals, axials, twists, and spins

In AAU competitions, costuming, showmanship, and audience appeal are not considered by the judge. Such elements are considered for a water show production because their presence entertains the audience.

The prospective judge is ready to practice judge routines after a study of the routine elements.

DESCRIPTION OF ROUTINE CATEGORIES

Failed   **Score: zero point**

Unless the cause is beyond the swimmer's control, a failed routine is one that progresses into the water and is then discontinued by the swimmer or swimmers.

Deficient   **Score: .1 to 2.9 points**

1. *Execution* The figures, strokes, and parts are incorrectly executed with major weaknesses in strength, line, elevation, and timing. Because of poor stroking, the routine may lap the pool only twice and may not seem to move.
2. *Content* Synchronization of the routine is poor. Movements within the solo routines are unrelated to the tempo and rhythmical beat of the music. Members of the duet and/or team seldom execute simultaneously. Other construction elements are poor (creative action, fluidity, difficulty, and diversity). The choreography is repetitive and simply performed in a jerky, splashy manner. The flow of movement is interrupted by dead spots.

Unsatisfactory   **Score: 3.0 to 4.9 points**

1. *Execution* The swimmer is limited in fundamental skills so that the routine lacks propulsion. The three basic kicking patterns—flutter, scissor, and whip—are weak. Originals are simple and weak in control.
2. *Content* There is an attempt to swim the strokes and execute figures together and with the music. Synchronization begins well but dissipates

as the routine progresses. Variety is limited because the swimmers have not developed a vast repertoire of skills. The originals and hybrids are relatively simple.

Satisfactory   **Score: 5.0 to 6.9 points**

1. *Execution*   The swimmer shows greater ability to swim standard and/ or hybrid strokes. Strength, line, and elevation are satisfactory. Stable figure positions are in line and elevated to nearly maximum sustained height. The routine moves throughout the pool, lapping it three or more times.

2. *Content*   A great share of the choreography is synchronized with a partner and with the music. A variety of skills, several simple, a few difficult, are used. The creative action adds interest and life to the performance. Movements tend to flow together.

Good   **Score: 7.0 to 8.9 points**

1. *Execution*   The strokes are strong, clean, elevated, and timed throughout. The figures and originals are in line, difficult or simple. The routine moves, covering the pool several times.

2. *Content*   The elements of content are outstanding. Synchronization is seldom lost. The choreography is filled with difficult, interesting movements. The flow of action is constant and complements each musical phrase. An abundance of creative movements add a superior quality to the routine.

Excellent   **Score: 9.0 to 10 points**

1. *Execution*   Perfection describes the execution of the figures, strokes, and parts thereof. Perfection is attained by powerful, confident, and expertly trained athletes.

2. *Content*   Synchronization above and below the water is nearly perfect. The routine moves rapidly with clean, precise action, making use of each downbeat of the music. The multiplicity of the routine choreography provides an air of the spectacular. All movements are controlled in an effortless manner. The performance is nearly flawless. The choreography is difficult. The routine laps the pool many times as the swimmers flow in and out of geometric patterns that are spaced and vividly focused. (The latter applies to team routines.) There is a trend in the duet event to synchronize figures and parts of figures, using propulsion sculling for flow of surface action. Few, if any, strokes are a part of the choreography. The duet event is rapidly becoming a synchronized figure routine.

We encourage participation in judging synchronized swimming. As the sport grows, it is in need of more nationally rated officials who represent all areas of the United States. We suggest the readers of this text become involved in training clinics, study the films that are available, and attend all levels of competition. Grow in your knowledge of the sport as our youth continue to increase their participation.

Following the suggested preparation for the judging of competitive synchronized swimming, only a few ingredients need to be added. Those are unbiased evaluations, ethical conduct, respect for the athletes in this competition, and a sincere love of the sport.

University of Michigan "Michifish" Club

10

THE WATER SHOW

FRAMEWORK FOR THE PRODUCTION

The first requisite of a successful water show is to be found in the clearly defined positive goals that give rise to the production. All aims of the sponsoring group must be kept in a proper perspective. The single most important purpose of any production should be to provide individuals with a sound educational experience that will contribute to the growth and development of their total personalities. Other secondary purposes include (1) the raising of funds both to support group participation in competitive meets and to purchase needed costumes and equipment, and (2) the public relations or informative purposes of the sponsoring institution.

Goals that the water show experience should provide group members are as follows:

1. Challenging the creative, imaginative, and inventive potentials of individuals by providing them with a variety of opportunities.
2. Providing a permissive environment for self-expression and free exchange of ideas, where logical reasoning, judgment, and discrimination can be developed.
3. Encouraging group experiences through which students may acquire a greater capacity for democratic attitudes of tolerance, sharing, and recognition of equality and dignity of the individual.

4. Motivating individual participants to work to their maximum abilities in all areas of endeavor.

5. Helping each individual to recognize and accept his limitations as well as his potentials.

6. Stressing the importance of the individual's worth by developing proper attitudes toward the value of his contribution to the group, thus enhancing his feeling of importance, belonging, and being accepted by his peers.

7. Providing evaluation periods to determine strengths and weaknesses.

8. Creating an awareness of personal satisfaction that comes from individual achievement.[1]

When the goals are reached, the following worthwhile values are achieved by everyone who participated: self-confidence, self-discipline, dedication, sacrifice, hard work and challenge, understanding of people, and fulfillment. The social goals are friendship with individuals and coaches, attainment of personal and team goals, sharing the fun and satisfaction of working toward and attaining goals and companionship with those who enjoy synchronized swimming.

The director of the water show must strive to accomplish these goals with the ultimate values in mind. While striving to provide guidance and leadership, he must contribute to the individual being, complete the organizational tasks, and add to the creative flavor with encouragement and enthusiasm. This is a responsibility of great proportions. The director must dedicate hours, days, and weeks of time to the fulfillment of the water show goals, values, and purposes. If, after the show is over, the director can say "It was worth it," the production was a success.

Selecting Swimmers for Synchronized Swimming Clubs

Of prime importance for a synchronized swimming club is obtaining swimmers whose skills meet the standard set by the club. However, before the swimmers are selected, the club director will need to consider how many swimmers the program and pool will accommodate. Secondly, how many coaches are available to teach the swimmers? Thirdly, what are the ultimate goals of the club or organization (water show, competition, or both)? And fourth, what skill levels and achievement levels are expected to be accomplished?

Individual clubs are free to set requirements that are suitable for their particular goals. A standard level of performance must be established and made available to those who wish to try out. The generally accepted method used to qualify swimmers for club membership is by administration of a skill test.

[1] Ferne Price, *Water Ballet Pageants* (Minneapolis, Minn.: Burgess Publishing Co., 1965).

This test should be composed of the basic skills needed for a synchronized swimmer, a satisfactory degree of proficiency in:

1. executing basic strokes
2. executing stable positions (chapter 3)
3. executing basic sculling for propulsion and support (chapter 4)
4. underwater swimming
5. executing basic figures and transitions (chapter 5)
6. feeling the rhythm when combining swimming strokes to a musical accompaniment

When preparing a skill test, be certain to test for these basic skills. Don't make the test so difficult that no one can pass it. Specifically, we suggest the test includes fundamental skills (refer to chapter 2), forms of sculling, underwater swim, identification and execution of three stable positions and three schooled figures (degree of difficulty, 1.5 to 1.7). The testing process should not be too long or time-consuming. Skills that go together may be combined, or short sequences of movements may be employed to keep the test short. The method and rating form for evaluating the prospective swimmers should be as simple as possible, and the testing should be done by experienced swimmers who are trained to recognize the acceptable skill level and who are capable of making judgements. It should be noted at this point that the average swimmer needs a starting place. Perhaps the skill test is that beginning. When a swimmer shows some degree of proficiency in the six basic skills, is enthusiastic and extremely interested in participation, she will undoubtedly meet the challenge of a water show besides acquiring new techniques and improving her skill while participating.

Most high schools and colleges provide preseason clinics to acquaint prospective members with the club organization, membership, and those skills necessary for the final tryouts. Often the clinics are conducted by the coach or present club members. Those members who have been previously trained in the necessary skills and teaching progressions enjoy such participation and teach effectively during clinics. When several clinics are planned, the coach should review teaching progressions with the teaching members prior to each clinic. Clinics should begin with the fundamental skills and build to the more difficult (see chapter 2).

Effective clinics employ the use of teaching stations. Several teachers are assigned to designated areas of the pool; each area is assigned specific skills; one demonstrator is needed at each station. Equal time should be maintained at each station, and students should rotate from station to station until they return to the starting point.

With a minimum amount of training, the present club membership may also judge the skill test given to new members. Such tests may be given at stations around the pool where one, two, or three judges are testing one or two skills. The swimmer being tested may begin at any station and rotate around the pool, with individual score sheets following the swimmers. Scores are recorded at all stations and computed for the final score.

Teaching Skills

The first part of this text presents a method of teaching synchronized swimming skills. The authors believe this method should be used for all levels of synchronized swimming groups. Swimmers will progress under this concept, becoming capable of assisting one another. The only limitations on any method of teaching and training are, of course, the physical situations of limited pool time and the number of available qualified coaches.

Student Directors

Swimmers should be given every opportunity to demonstrate leadership, responsibility, and creativity in choreography and routine direction. Selection of these swimmers, called student directors, should be based on their interest, skill, creativity, and abilities to relate to their peers. With proper supervision, the student director's total contribution should be an asset to the production. Student directors will need to identify with their responsibilities and meet deadlines. Primarily, they are responsible for a group routine and do not swim in the routine they direct. The soloists, duets, and trios usually report their progress and problems to the coach since they are generally skilled swimmers capable of choreographing their own routines. This is also true in competitive clubs; however, the teams usually have a parent who coordinates the details with the coach.

SUGGESTED RESPONSIBILITIES FOR STUDENT DIRECTORS

1. Select music and routine theme; seek approval of coach.
2. Research theme extensively.
3. Choreograph routine.
4. Become familiar with the skills of the swimmers; stay within their skill range.
5. Develop an original beginning and ending for the routine.
6. Choreograph something original in the routine.
7. Teach arm, leg, and head movements.
8. Establish group practices; keep attendance.
9. Inform coach of progress and difficulties.
10. Always make effective use of pool time.
11. Be organized for each practice; review and progress to new material.

12. Critique routines at all practices and dress rehearsals.

13. Be cognizant of operation and care of all audio equipment.

14. Write an appropriate narrative based on factual material and give it to an appropriate person before deadline dates.

15. Research and design costumes; give designs to appropriate persons by deadline dates.

16. When students are making their own costumes, organize procedures.

17. With the director's knowledge or consent, delegate purchases for costumes and materials.

18. Progress the routine according to established schedules (routines must be show ready one week in advance).

19. Pool safety dictates a senior lifesaver or water-safety instructor be on deck at all times.

Student directors are effective and highly responsible when they are aware of their obligations. They can contribute to the democratic atmosphere and general enthusiasm for the total production.

Theme and Title Selection

THEME

A water show needs a theme: a foundation and a framework of routines that create its shape and identity. Future planning and show continuity is developed out of a broad, flexible, and workable theme, or show idea, which can be broken down into significant parts, or subthemes, for routines.

The show theme should be determined democratically; all interested cast members should be given the opportunity to express their ideas freely. Often it is more expedient to appoint a theme selection committee that solicits ideas from the group, meets to explore and develop these ideas, and finally reports the ideas to the total group for selection. When the group consists of junior high school age swimmers with limited experience, the coach may choose to select the theme.

When making the final selection of the water show theme, members should first consider the ability to portray the theme and its appeal to the general public, young and old; the availability of money and props; and the adaptability of the theme to the physical facilities surrounding the pool. When the majority of the group is excited over a theme, interest is stimulated toward creative routine development, and the idea has enough potential to be a success. Here are some further guidelines to consider in theme selection:

1. Toward total show continuity, the theme should suggest routines, music, narrative, and staging.

2. To tie the production together, it should suggest an appropriate opening number and finale.

3. It should suggest routines that add variety to the show—novelty and special-effects routines as well as light, romantic, impressionistic, and dramatic ones.

4. The theme ideas should be creative, timely, flexible, and broad, and geared to the ages of the group.

5. Themes should be neither too commonplace nor topical, as an idea is often better after it has aged.

TITLE

The title is the distinguishing name given to the production and should suggest the theme and add continuity to the performance. It should be short, clever, catchy, appealing, an alliteration, and/or a play on words. Some examples are: "Street Beats," "Visions of Future Passed," "Aqua Scenium," "A Touch of Frost," "Myth or Miracle," and "People, People, People." The title is largely a part of the publicity; its characteristics should help sell the show. Every member of the cast should be given the opportunity to select the title. One that has been researched and carefully thought out usually stands the best chance of selection; research not only stimulates the individual's participation but also broadens the show's potential.

Casting the Show

Following the selection of the theme and title, the swimmers are cast in routines in which it is thought they have the ability to make their best contribution to the theme. This is a difficult task because swimmers are sensitive to the choices that must be made. The coach, assistant coach, and president of the club usually participate in the making of these decisions. To foster good will, the criteria used in casting should be understood by the cast. Strong consideration should be given to the following: experience and skill, sense of rhythm, swimming style, tenure of membership in the club, physical and personality characteristics, and compatibility with others.

Swimmers should be given opportunity to submit their first, second, and third choice of a routine; those with whom they would like to swim; and the routine they feel able and willing to direct. All this information is kept confidential by the coach. The final decisions are seldom based entirely on the choices submitted by the swimmers; however, in knowing there was an attempt to please, the students will generally accept the final outcome and pledge their loyalty.

When an AAU competitive club presents its annual water show, the routine swimmers have usually been selected according to skill and age, with some emphasis on physical compatibility. The decisions are the responsibility of the coach.

The number of swimmers per routine is important. The coach is guided by the fact that the more people swimming in a routine, the more difficult it is to synchronize. It follows, therefore, that the more-skilled swimmers should be in the large numbers, the less-skilled swimmers in smaller-group numbers (clever choreography can facilitate simple skills), and the better-skilled swimmers in the duets, trios, and solos. Large-group numbers should be composed of swimmers who have a good sense of rhythm but who are not necessarily able to perform difficult schooled figures (figures of 1.4 to 1.7 degree of difficulty).

It is also helpful for swimmers of trios, duets, and solos to be aware of the criteria for selecting these combinations:

1. The skill level and experience warrants first consideration.
2. Solos are given to outstanding, experienced swimmers capable of exceptional skill, execution, and interpretation of the music.[2]
3. Outstanding skill and compatibility, as well as similar style and physical characteristics, are given emphasis when selecting duets and trios.
4. Group swimmers are selected on the basis of equal skill. They must be capable of rising to the challenge of more difficult skills within their reach.
5. When possible, small groups should be average in skill, capable of presenting enough talent to hold the attention of the audience.
6. Swimmers are placed in group routines according to their ability to handle the choreography and remain synchronized. When exceptional skill and showmanship are added, the audience will be well pleased.
7. When possible, swimmers are assigned to the "star" positions based on dedication and number of years devoted to the club. When there are prestigious routines (perhaps of less skill), such as coeducation duets, coeducational group routines, and special-effects routines, the coach should use the persons who have dedicated themselves and served several years.
8. The routine alternate is considered a prestigious position. The alternate should be given the opportunity to swim in at least one performance.
9. Sometimes age difference between swimmers is used for special characterization.
10. A contrast in physical characteristics may determine the selection of swimmers for unique roles.
11. General health, physical stamina, class load, and extracurricular activities must be considered in selecting swimmers for routines that make greater demands.

[2] Price, *Water Ballet Pageants.*

Probably the most important product of a water show production is the attitude formed by the total group during and after swimming and working together. The production is a success when it creates a friendly, cooperative attitude, swimmer to swimmer, officer to officer, swimmer to officer, director to coach, cast to crew, and crew to director. When good attitudes prevail, high-level performance results in a professional show that will be thoroughly enjoyed by the audience and those who made it possible.

Program and Listed Order of Routines

PROGRAM

Since the printed program is the first item to greet the audience, its design should project the overall theme at a glance. This is generally accomplished through an artistic design (relating to the general theme) that helps convey the intended idea of each routine. Programs for productions should give correct and necessary information, as well as look professional, neat, and attractive.

It is highly recommended that one person coordinate all aspects of the printed program. Items which must be considered are: cover design, selection of a printer, content (acknowledgements, names of members, officers and coaches, committees, technical staff, and advertisers) deadline dates, and proofreading of the program.

The program coordinator should begin soon after the title is selected. An artist should be chosen who will create an appropriate design that is attractive and related to the general theme. (To be consistent and practical, the same design can be used for the advertising.) The size and shape of the program must be determined before the artist begins work, as these dictate the scale for the drawing. After the design is selected, a school or community printer should be consulted to determine a cost estimate for the cover sheet and the number of inserts. Certain information will need to be agreed upon by the coordinator and the printer, such as paper weight and color, ink colors, number of pages, quantity needed, and date required. It is wise to seek cost estimates from several sources before selecting the best competitive bid. To prevent errors, it is recommended that the program be carefully proofread before it goes to print. This is also the last opportunity to make unforeseen changes and correc-tions. The program coordinator must submit the necessary information to the printer in time to meet the production dates. Whenever possible, the printed program should be available for the first dress rehearsal as its use will help cue the cast during rehearsal.

The program should include:

1. Title
2. Place
3. Time and dates
4. Titles of numbers, listed in order of performance

5. Names of performers in alphabetical order
6. Choreographers
7. Names of members in organizations, including officers and coaches
8. Committees, chairmen, and assistants
9. Acknowledgments
10. Other information, such as advertising, history of club, and dedication

ORDER OF ROUTINES

The order of the routines should be determined well in advance of the printing. Generally, it should be a logical sequence that not only helps develop the theme and continuity of the routines but also appeals to the audience. When establishing a routine order, the time needed by the performers for costume changes should be considered. Performers should not be placed in two consecutive routines and should be given at least one, preferably two, routines in which to change. To prevent quick costume changes, use continuity skits that will enhance the theme of the show. Other important considerations for the order of routines are:

1. The production should begin with a routine that stimulates attention, is unique and original, and sets the stage for the entire production.
2. For balance, arrange the numbers by mood and music tempo.
3. Solos, duets, trios, and team routines should be spaced to add variety and balance.
4. Entrances and exits should be varied.
5. The special-effects routines should be dramatically spaced.
6. Routines with highly skilled swimmers should be used to lead to the climatic finish, whereas lesser-skilled swimming routines should be properly spaced throughout.
7. The production should include a variety of selections: novelty and comedy routines as well as dramatic, impressionistic, inspirational, light, gay, and romantic selections.
8. Intermission entertainment could include comedy diving, a demonstration on the trampoline, fancy diving, or a special dance group.
9. Routines should be arranged to allow for a production lasting one to one and a half hours. Because bleacher seating is uncomfortable, a production of greater length is not recommended.
10. The production should build toward a climactic finale, which should include the entire cast and be made simple enough so that all may be synchronized with the music. The finale should be dramatic, related to the theme, and should tie the whole performance together, leaving the audience with a feeling of wanting to see more.[3]

[3] Ibid.

The Practice Schedule

Practice makes perfect is a meaningful adage only when an effective practice plan is in operation, one that is known to result in marked improvement among the participants.

Practice for the water show should begin six to eight weeks prior to the production. This means that all routines must be choreographed and ready for both land and water sessions with the music by this time.

To comply with the proposed beginning of practice, all choreographers should begin composition some two to three weeks ahead of the first set date. To assist the choreographer in organizing her time, a guide is suggested in terms of deadline dates for completion of the first third, second third, and the total routine. Another date may be given for completion of the deck movements and entry into the water.

Within the high school and college environs, one student director for each team routine is responsible for organizing and conducting practice of her show number. Emphasis should be placed on practice in the water as often as possible, preceded by walk through rehearsals on deck. The student director may begin her group practice by playing the music for the team members, followed by a discussion of the theme interpretation. The musical tempo should be identified along with the rhythmical count of two, four, eight, or three, six, nine.

The choreography is best taught on land in segments (completed sequences after traversing one lap of the pool). This plan aids rapid learning. Also, to assist the team member, enough cassette tape recordings should be made so that each member may take a copy home for practice.

When the swimmers move to the water, all routine parts are tried very slowly, followed by an explanation of the techniques of execution. If parts seem not to fit, land practice is resumed and the problems resolved. This procedure from land to water to land is followed until the routine parts are polished.

The less-skilled groups will require more coaching time to insure a commendable performance. The head coach should schedule additional rehearsals for those whose need is greatest. The coach is in charge of these sessions; a student director should not be expected to sacrifice an overabundance of study time.

We recommend that two or three routines practice at the same time, alternating pool space with the use of the music. For example, routine A is in the water with the music while routine B is walking through its choreography. Routine C is in the water along the pool side practicing team originals and hybrids under the guidance of the student director. When routine A has concluded, members of this team go to a designated corner to listen to the taped critique. Routine B makes use of the water and music with a critic watching who has a second cassette recorder. At the conclusion of routine B, all routines shift places. A goes into the water along side the pool to improve the errors in execution. B goes to the corner for its critique, and C swims the routine with the music and a recorded critique. The recommended order for the practice of three routines is to move the groups from the water with music, to the critique, to the water for improvement of errors.

Frequency of practice without great intervals between sessions is best for progress. One hour twice a week per routine is minimum. Scheduling is difficult because of lack of available pool time and swimmers' personal schedules. However, when possible, practice should be arranged in blocks of three to four hours.

A practice schedule should be posted at least two weeks in advance so that swimmers have time to adjust their activities calendars. Hopefully, absenteeism can be kept minimal, but it is also a good policy to train an alternate swimmer. She should be expected to attend all rehearsals and swim along side the regulars.

The quality of the show is subject to the general goals of the club and the amount of practice time students are able to give. If practice has been started eight to ten weeks before the show, there should be no reason to add long and tiring rehearsals the last two weeks. The last few remaining practices should give emphasis to spacing, focus, deck movements, head movements, and facial expressions.

Tickets

A ticket serves as evidence that the holder has paid to see the performance and is guaranteed a seat. It conveys to the holder vital information regarding the performance: place, time, date, name of the event, and price of admission.

A ticket committee handles both printing and distribution of the tickets. A meeting of this committee should be set at least two months prior to the performance to determine the ticket price, design, and color. A plan for the distribution of the tickets should be agreed upon and a deadline set for the return of unsold tickets as well as the money from the sale of tickets.

The ticket committee must determine the seating capacity and, from this information, authorize the number of tickets to be printed. To defray the cost of printing the ticket, an appropriate commercial ad may appear on the back of the ticket—promoting the local sports shop, for example.

To foster good public relations, a complimentary ticket list should be handed to the ticket chairman in advance of ticket distribution. The coach should serve as the clearing house for such a list. Special groups from the surrounding area may include a children's home, under-privileged children from the county welfare, YWCA and handicapped children. Other persons from the community and from departments within the school who assisted in some phase of the production should be sent a complimentary ticket. It is customary to include on the list, through a letter of invitation, school administrators, faculty, advertisers, and other community leaders. We suggest the complimentary ticket list be kept at a minimum because seating is usually limited in swimming pools. The paid audience must be given priority if the performance is to show a profit.

The distribution and sale of tickets requires an organized plan tenaciously adhered to by the person in charge. We recommend the following plan:

1. Use a different color ticket for each performance.
2. Issue a select number of tickets for each performance to those persons responsible for ticket sales.
3. Place tickets for each performance in a separate envelope; for example: three performances, three envelopes.
4. Label each envelope as follows: name, number of tickets, number sold, number returned, total money.

At the conclusion of the preticket sale, each envelope should be sealed, the information provided as requested on the front of the envelope, and the sealed contents given to the ticket chairman. The chairman, at her convenience, should record the sales, giving accurate credit to each person who sold tickets. (When a ticket contest is held, the prize winner may be acknowledged at an appropriate time.) All unsold tickets must be returned several hours before the performance, enabling the chairman to know what is available for sale at the door.

The ticket chairman should designate a time and place for her sales force to pick up or return tickets. This schedule should accommodate the group to the best advantage.

Monies from door sales at each performance should be added to the preticket sale for that performance. These statistics provide the coach with information regarding the most popular night and capacity crowds.

A final financial report should be presented to the show director and president of the swim club.

Publicity

Publicity is the technique of attracting public attention to a production. The success of the water show depends on the exposure given to the production by the publicity chairman and her committee. The committee must be creative and use good taste in developing promotional techniques. Publicity should give a purpose and an explanation, plus additional information necessary to stimulate public interest. In addition, the time, place, dates, price, title, and sale of tickets need to be included.

The timing of the publicity plays a large role in its effectiveness. First announcements should begin about three weeks prior to the production. The bulk of the promotion begins two weeks in advance and peaks two or three days before the first performance.

PROMOTIONAL IDEAS

1. The sale of tickets is promoted through the interest and enthusiasm generated by the entire cast. When the cast is knowledgeable and excited over their roles in the production, they will be effective salesmen.

2. A catchy title with well-designed posters attracts attention.

3. Fliers should be mailed to surrounding schools announcing the performance. Mailing should occur three weeks in advance, thus allowing schools the necessary time for making arrangements to attend the production. The appearance of the fliers should be neat and professional.

4. Attractive posters and fliers should be posted in the community grocery stores, gas stations, restaurants, drug stores, churches and schools, apartment buildings, house and car windows, and other areas of notice to the local population.

5. Local radio stations generally promote club activities. Usually, a postcard listing all information concerning the production is all that is needed for an announcement. Information should be sent two weeks prior to the production. Personal interviews by radio or TV stations will need to be scheduled earlier.

6. Local TV stations will promote productions through the showing of video tapes, if such tapes have been prepared far enough in advance to meet the TV schedule. The video taping session should be used exclusively for this purpose. Do not attempt to tape during a dress rehearsal or weekly practice, as the sound and lighting will generally need adjustments.

7. Articles and pictures in newspapers enhance publicity. Articles must be well-written, and the readers should be given only enough information to stimulate their interest. If your area is served by more than one newspaper, submit different articles to the individual papers.

8. Pictures are tremendous for promotion, as they give a visual idea of the show. Some local newspapers send their own photographers, while others ask to have pictures submitted. Special photographing sessions will need to be arranged. Pictures are more interesting when performers are posed in costume either on deck or in the water. However, because refraction creates difficulty when taking pictures in the water, deck poses may be preferable. When an underwater window is available, posed underwater photos are of great interest.

9. A flower or corsage given to the swimmers after a dress rehearsal is a reward to the cast and acts as advertising for the coming production.

10. Public address systems within the schools, camps, and clubs should be used to announce the production.

11. Good public relations can be further established at the conclusion of the production when the publicity committee removes all posters, pictures, etc. A variety of publicity methods should be encouraged, as the more promotion there is meeting the public eye, the better the opportunities of attracting a large audience. Be creative with promotional ideas, but by all means promote the show in good taste.

Narration and Narrator

A narration that serves its intended purpose has three major accomplishments: it interprets the central theme, sets the stage for each individual routine, and adds continuity to the entire production. The narration is developed through research that covers all aspects of the theme so that the audience is given an authentic accounting. Because the creation of an interesting narration is a time-consuming activity for one person, each student director is requested to research her routine with the intent of supplying the narrator with sufficient information.

The narration should follow guidelines. To open the show, the overall theme is introduced in a manner that whets the appetite of the audience for what is to come and follows with a smooth entry into the introduction of the first routine. All narration that precedes the individual routines (except the opening and closing numbers) should be short and to the point (maximum thirty seconds) unless longer periods are necessary for costume changes. The script should contain humor and some dramatic emphasis. Every effort should be made to tie each routine into the central theme. Finally, the narration should conclude in a manner that will encourage the audience to attend next year's production. To allow the narrator adequate practice time, the script should be completed at least three weeks prior to the performance.

The selection of a capable narrator is extremely important. The smoothness of the show often depends on the alertness of the person at the mike. Specific desirable qualities of a narrator are stage poise, a speaking voice of pleasing quality, the ability to stay in character, familiarity with the activity, the ability to ad-lib during unexpected gaps, and a conscientious attitude.

The script should never sound as if it is being read; it should be delivered in a conversational manner. As in play acting, the narrator speaks the lines directly to the audience. When this is done, all attention will be directed to the narrator and what is being said. Such a captivated audience will not be aware of the movement of the cast in the shadows. To add to the spirit and character of the show, the narrator may appear in different locations, appear in different costumes or use different props. Such maneuvers must be practiced to prevent mix-ups in lighting and sound.

If circumstances make it advisable, the narration may be recorded on tape. In that case, care must be taken to produce a clear, articulate delivery of words and thought so that the voice on tape is modulated at a level that is readily understood throughout the natatorium. To augment the speaking parts in a show, many productions make use of creative visual aids such as slides or movies. Such techniques are effective when the picture is dilated to adequate proportions for the entire audience to see.

TECHNICAL ASPECTS OF THE PRODUCTION

Sound Systems and Recordings

High quality sound equipment must be given top priority over all other equipment. The audience and the performers must be able to hear the music and understand the speaking voices. The equipment needed generally includes a microphone, record player, tape recorder, underwater speakers, an amplifier, and air speakers. This equipment may be rented when otherwise unavailable within the school or university. Greatest efficiency in production of sound comes from matching the components to the complete system. Sound system experts should be consulted to obtain the best results from the available equipment.

The use of the same equipment for rehearsals and the production is a must, as speed control varies from one machine to another. In cases of an emergency, a back-up sound system should be made available for immediate use. Underwater speakers are extremely valuable for all synchronized swimming activities. These speakers also need to be used during practice to accustom performers to the underwater sound.

Information pertaining to top-quality sound systems that are available today may be obtained by contacting the Jole Company and/or Lubell Laboratories Incorporated, both of which have provided the sound for National AAU Synchronized Swimming Championships and/or Midwest Intercollegiate meets.

The person operating the sound system should be well-trained in handling the equipment and be very familiar with the music cues during the progress of the show. The music technician must be sensitive to good quality in music and know when the volume is just right for each performance, rehearsals, and final productions. An unpleasing quality of sound is annoying and distracting; therefore, both the volume and a mixture of instruments should be adjusted for clarity and richness. The sound technician should establish the correct settings during rehearsals; however, adjustments may be needed during the performance because an audience will absorb some of the sound. Such changes may be made during the first number.

The sound technician should be expected to prepare a show tape, one that separates each routine by a white leader of a few seconds. The show tape can be on two reels: the first reel includes all the music up to the intermission; the second includes the music following intermission through the finale.

Tapes and tape recorders are most often used for high school and college water show productions. Therefore, to aid those persons in charge of tape making, we offer the following guidelines. When superior-quality recordings are desired, the tapes should be made at a professional studio where the room is sound proofed and the music is fed directly from the record player into the tape recorder (not picked up from a microphone). Expensive studio equipment provides top quality in tone and regulated volume. Editing and splicing is quickly and easily done by the use of monitors that assist in finding the actual note and moment in tempo. These tapes are free from splice noise and are balanced in volume (the highs are lowered and the soft parts brought up). It is also possible to add echo to a splice that otherwise is abrupt. Such advantages amply compensate for the fee charged.

Time and money are saved by preplanning the recording session at the studio. First, while at home, edit the music by notation on paper; play the length of each segment of music and time it with a stop watch. Write down the length of time, the name of the music or record, and the band number. Describe the actual cut by identifying the instruments, the rhythmical count, the volume, and any other meaningful characteristics. Having prepared all this at home, there is less margin for error and less time spent at the studio.

Taping should be completed before the practice sessions begin. Usually two identical tapes are made, one for practice and the other saved for dress rehearsal and the actual show. Practice tapes do deteriorate in quality because they pick up a hiss sound as they are played over and over. Also, there is great chance in breakage, stretch, or a fold in the tape when winding.

To save money, many groups assign an amateur the job of recording the music for the show. In this case, the following equipment is needed: two good-quality tape recorders (not push button) with a quick-stop lever, a record player equipped with a new needle (variable speed), patch cords, splicer and splicing tape, razor blade, stop watch, and a soft colored pencil. Also vital is the possession of a good ear for music. For best results when recording music, use seven and one-half speed. Connect the record player to the tape recorder and feed the sound directly into the tape recorder. Quality is lost when sound is picked up from a microphone.

Determine the volume desired by watching the arrow in the record dial. Volume that forces the black arrow into the red area will be distorted when played back. Always record extra music on the tape before and after the splice. This will allow room to cut out the pop, or noise, from the "on" and "off" switch.

Generally, tape recorders have two heads. One head located to the right of the recording mechanism serves as both the *record* and *playback* head. A second head, located to the left of the record area, is the *erase* head. It is helpful to the amateur to identify these heads so that there is less margin of error when marking the cut with the soft yellow pencil.

A clean cut at the end of a melody usually results after marking the tape to the right of the playback head. The location of this mark is determined after stopping the machine just after the last note, including the echo, is heard.

To mark the beginning of a melody, play that section of the music several times beginning at 000 on the numerical meter dial. Watch the dial and identify the number and its position just prior to hearing the beginning of the music. Stop the machine at this point and place a yellow dot or dash across the tape to the left of the playback head. Free the tape by manually turning the reels. Locate both yellow marks on the tape. With a razor blade, cut the tape diagonally across the yellow marks. Ease the two tape ends together, matching the cuts as you would match pieces of a jigsaw puzzle. Firmly press the splicing tape over the splice. Use the back of the thumbnail to press the air out of the splice. Play the splice through the machine and check it for consistency in tempo. All splices must be made with as little tempo change as possible, unless the new melody is preceded by a bridge of music (introductory run or a transition that serves the same purpose). Label each completed tape and mark its length in minutes and seconds according to the stop watch. Splice a white leader to the beginning, and wind the tape onto a left reel for immediate playback. Allow plenty of time for the editing of tape music. Such an effort requires knowledge of music, rhythm, and extreme patience.

Cassettes have been a boon to synchronized swimming. Some of the more expensive cassette recorders will play reel tapes and cartridges. The cartridge combines the best features: it is less expensive to use, fast to rewind, quick to change, fairly durable, and easily portable. This equipment is readily used for practice sessions on deck, but not for tapes to be used during the show.

Because the acoustics in many swimming pools are inadequate, when speaking parts are used, they must be slow and more distinct than usual. The use of a microphone will amplify the voice. However, microphones are known to have different degrees of sensitivity; therefore, the narrator must practice speaking into the microphone while standing or holding the mike at a satisfactory distance from the mouth. The music technician must set the proper volume control for the voice. Because it is annoying for an audience to see someone speaking and not be able to hear the sound, or worse, to have the sound blast out, we recommend all adjustments be determined before dress rehearsal.

Sometimes the voice is recorded directly on the master tape. When this method is followed, a spotlight focuses on scenery or props, directing the attention of the audience to that point. During this time, the cast is able to make exists and entrances safely but unnoticed.

Music and sounds may also be provided by a live orchestra or a talented combo. Be certain that each rehearses in the pool to determine its effectiveness.

Moderate to soft sounds may be used to set a mood during the arrival and departure of the spectators. Because good music and sound are essential to a good water show, it is important that the director assume responsibility for securing the best possible sound.

In conclusion, we caution against the careless use of electrical equipment, wires, and plugs around the pool. All such items must be double-checked for defects. To ensure the safety of the performers and technicians, take every precaution necessary to comply with electrical codes.

Costumes

Because the water show is a series of successive acts, there is great opportunity to create good first impressions through costuming. Hence, an exceptional costume attracts attention and interest, whereas an unsuitable or unattractive costume handicaps a performer from making a good impression.[4] A costume should not only look good on the performer but also be styled to portray the routine theme or character. It should be lightweight, comfortable for swimming, durable, adaptable to the water medium, carry out the theme, and designed attractively and appropriately, having a good line and in good taste.

Costumes for synchronized swimming usually begin with a basic bathing suit. The front of the bathing suit is seen more often by the audience; therefore, it deserves more attention than the back. Furthermore, because some part of the head is always in the spotlight, it deserves the greatest attention. Covering the hands, legs, and feet should be avoided, for this adds weight to the performer, making swimming more difficult. However, some accessories on the arms and legs enhance the costume and can be worn without adverse effect. Trimmings are effective when they are vivid in design, color, and texture. Stylized designs are more suitable than complicated designs of intricate detail and perhaps less expensive for water show costumes (expense is generally a concern).

Materials used for costumes must be waterproof and durable. Some recommended fabrics are: lamés, eyelash, nylon netting, lace, synthetic satin and velvet, bathing suit fabrics, jersey, and oilcloth. Other modern fabrics can be used; however, they should be water-tested and dried before cutting the pattern. Materials that reflect light, lamés and eyelash, are very effective and appealing to an audience.

To accent the theme, suits may be decorated and trimmed with durable and waterproof items. Recommended trims are: waterproof sequins (sequins sprayed with a clear waterproof substance), braiding and rickrack, jewels, buttons, costume jewelry, plastics, nylon-velvet ribbon, pearls, rhinestones, beads, nylon netting, satin, plastic flowers, and plastic doilies.

The use of color, a vivid design for trim, and the texture of fabrics are important concerns in stylizing the bathing suit. Varying with each routine, colors should be symbolic and/or realistic, providing interesting contrast. Colors may be combined to create harmony within the design and enhance the overall effect. Colors can portray feelings: pale colors indicate lightness in mood; bright colors (red, yellow, orange) indicate gaiety and intensity, whereas dark colors indicate royalty or somberness. Care should be taken in designing swimming costumes for duets or teams so that all look alike. Kim Welshon, former AAU national champion, suggests the following steps.

[4] Beulah Gundling and Peg Seller, *Aquatic Art* (Cedar Rapids, Iowa: Pioneer Litho Co., 1957).

Steps in Designing a Costume

1. Determine the theme of your routine.
2. Research the idea to obtain the proper details for the costume. (Research from libraries, magazines, books, TV, authentic costumes, movies, ice follies, and dance programs.)
3. Select a suit. This can be a basic tank suit, a suit purchased from a store, one made from a pattern, or a leotard. The fabric selection must be carefully considered: the color is important to the theme; the weight must be light so as not to hamper the swimmer.
4. Decorate and trim the suit to accent the theme.
5. Create a headpiece that coordinates with the suit in carrying out the theme. The headpiece should be simple, small, lightweight, and like a sieve (to allow water to flow through freely).
6. The costume should have several trial swims, assuring a well-designed, comfortable suit and headpiece.[5]

Bathing suits may be ordered from most bathing suit supply houses at a club discount. These orders need to be placed three months in advance to assure delivery by the specified dates.

The aesthetic importance of the headpiece has already been mentioned. Its structure is best accomplished by the trial and error method to obtain the proper effect, as well as a comfortable fit that allows for ease of swimming. The materials used for the construction of the headpiece frame are most often household screen (aluminum or copper) and/or eighteen-gauge galvanized wire (heavy), or beading wire. Various sizes of household sieves and the bowl-shaped screens from flour sifters are ideal frames for hats.) After the desired shape is designed, it may then be spray-painted or covered with fabric for the desired color. When screening has been cut to shape, seam tape must be sewn or stapled around the rough edges. The design may be further styled by the trims and decorations previously enumerated. For swimmers with short hair, the headpiece should be affixed to a nylon net (double or triple thickness) or a skullcap. Those with long hair may affix the hat to the hair. The hair must be specially styled in a bun or braids on the top or back of the head; bobby pins and hair combs must be used to keep the headpiece in place. Kim Welshon suggests the following steps in designing a headpiece:

1. Shape the headpiece from heavy papers. Try it on and make the necessary adjustments.

---

[5] *Synchro-Info,* 11902 Red Hill Avenue, Santa Ana, Calif., 92705. Vol. X, No. 4, August, 1972.

2. Pin the pattern onto two layers of screening and cut it out.
3. Place wire around all edges of screening and sew to screen with a zigzag stitch.
4. Brace whenever necessary with wire gauge that has been stitched (zigzag) to the screening.
5. Use seam tape on rough edges.
6. Spray paint or cover with material.
7. Decorate to coordinate with bathing suit.[6]

Kim also suggests attaching the headpiece to the hair by several different methods to insure against loss while swimming.

1. Use many bobby pins in an inconspicuous manner. Put them directly through a covered wire that has been added to the center of the headpiece or through wire "eyes" (large) sewn along the edge of the hat.
2. Hair pins through braided loops of hair may be bent at each end to secure the hat (a trick used by beauticians).
3. Use bobby pins through horsehair, attached to own hair.
   a. Cross the pins over each other for added reinforcement.
   b. Sew combs on the front, side, and back of the headpiece to prevent pulling.[7]

When the headpiece is attached to a nylon cap rather than the hair, it must be sewn on in the proper place on the cap. The cap style should allow one inch or more of the hair line in front to show, covering half of the ear. The cap should be made to fit like a glove. An elastic chin strap with an eye hook, or pin, will hold the cap in place. Many bobby pins (large size and unexposed) will be needed to hold the cap and headpiece in place during a routine. Swimmers will need to practice several times with their headpieces to become acquainted with their properties in regard to the water medium.

Costume designing is an exciting part of a water show. When all the costumes are completed for the dress rehearsal and seen for the first time under the spotlights, the cast is thrilled with its own first impressions. Later, their enthusiasm is readily transmitted to the audience.

ORGANIZATIONAL PLANS FOR DESIGNING AND CONSTRUCTING COSTUMES

For water shows or competition, costumes may be designed and constructed for the swimmers, or swimmers may make their own under the guidance of a knowledgeable person. Some type of organized system must be followed

[6] Ibid.
[7] Ibid.

to accomplish the desired outcomes. Budget, time, and the sewing skills of parents, swimmers, and coaches dictate the most effective system under which to operate. Three plans will be considered.

Plan one

Swimmers purchase and design their own costumes. The director designates the responsibility to one individual per routine, who, in turn, is responsible to the director.

Whenever swimmers are responsible for financing their costumes, they must be aware of the estimated cost per costume. Another consideration, when several persons are sewing, is to ensure that all costumes for each routine look alike; the fabric must all be cut from the same pattern and all trims sewn in the appropriate place. To create the acceptable costume design, there must be close communication between the director and costume persons. For cutting cost and waste, it is recommended that purchases be made in large quantities rather than each individual per routine making small purchases. To insure that costumes are sewn well and will last for all performances, we recommend further that each routine have a workshop for those persons making the costumes.

Plan two

Basic bathing suits are owned by the club. Each routine has a set budget of club monies, and a designated individual (swimmer or parent) is in charge of designing, purchasing, and distributing materials for each routine. This individual is directly responsible to the director; or, the director designs all costumes and cuts the patterns, and the parents and swimmers sew the costumes under the guidance of the director.

Following this plan, individual club members will not be required to finance their own costumes. This means, however, that the club will need to budget monies for this purpose. The club will eventually gain an inventory of suits and trims that can be used year after year. Eventually, storage space and an inventory will be needed to make good use of the supplies. As previously enumerated in plan one, good communications, workshops, and purchases in large quantities are necessary

Plan three

Basic suits and materials are supplied by the club, and a person is hired to design and sew all costumes. Without a doubt, this plan is the most efficient; however, since a larger costume budget is needed, many clubs will be unable to follow this pattern. When storage and inventory have been carefully attended to the previous year, the same basic suits and some trims can be reused; this cuts down on expenses. The cost is also reduced by having one person do the purchasing in large quantities. Hours of time for approval of costume designs are eliminated, since the communication lies between the director and the seamstress rather than the large number of persons required in plans one and two. This procedure also eliminates the need for workshops. Basically, this plan provides well-sewn costumes with many different designs. Of course, the primary difficulty with such a plan is locating a seamstress willing to undertake such a task.

As costumes are an integral part of a water show, so is the plan for purchase, design, construction, and sewing of the costumes. Any plan has advantages and disadvantages; the director must determine which plan has the greatest merit for each particular situation.

Lighting

Lighting creates a mood and transforms the natatorium into a stage upon which the swimmer becomes an artistic performer. Lighting cues the action to begin and directs the attention of the audience. Lighting is a form of communication between the performer and the audience. Its use gives meaning to the total production.

The lighting is subject to the artistic judgment and taste of the show director and her consultants. Because there is technical difficulty in lighting the water medium, we recommend that a skilled lighting technician be employed.

Perhaps the first obstacle in lighting is light refraction. The law of refraction is as follows: a ray of light passing into a denser medium is bent toward a perpendicular drawn to the surface at the point of entry. When it emerges into the less dense medium, it is bent away from the perpendicular drawn at that point.[8] Knowing these physical properties of light, it is possible to adequately light a water show production even though the light is passing into water and air, two different densities.

Good lighting will usually result from understanding and consideration of the following: the functions and qualities of the lights, the source of the lights, the lighting of the performers, lights for safety, colored lights, and special-effects equipment.

According to Parker and Smith, the functions of lighting are:

1. *Visibility:* You should see what is intended to be seen.
2. *Plasticity:* Create a reasonably accurate imitation of light that could naturally be seen.
3. *Composition:* Tie the stage picture together into a pleasing scene.
4. *Mood:* All of the above must be met to create the mood.[9]

Lighting has qualities as well as functions; they are:

1. *Intensity*—the brightness of the light
2. *Color*—all colors from the color spectrum

⁸ Oren W. Parker and Harvey Smith, *Scene Design and Stage Lighting* (New York and Chicago: Holt, Rinehart and Winston, Inc., 1963).
⁹ Ibid.

3. *Distribution*—the form and direction of the light
4. *Movement*—subtle or abrupt changes (The movement can be in color, intensity, or distribution.) [10]

Effective lighting should incorporate all of the functions and qualities of lighting to illuminate the performers, props, and scenery. These elements of lighting affect the atmosphere of the show and the artistic impact the performance will have on the audience.

Basically, there are two sources of light: direct sunlight and artificial light. For indoor water show productions, we are concerned with artificial lighting. Artificial light is produced by strong bulbs, arc lights, carbon arc lamps, follow spots, ultraviolet lamps, floods, underwater lights, and ceiling lights. Arc and carbon arc lamps are extremely expensive; therefore, we suggest the use of 1500 watt follow spots (trouperette spots) and less powerful floods. For ideal illumination, four of these spots, supplemented with flood lights, will adequately light a pool forty-five by seventy-five feet with a balcony that extends beyond both ends of the pool. When less than four spots are used, other light sources must be provided. The main concern is to provide sufficient light on the faces and bodies of the performers so that from any position in the balcony the spectator may clearly see the action without the interference of shadows.

To properly light the performers, straight-ahead lighting is not recommended, as it washes out the performer's face, making it appear as an expressionless mask. It is best to light from a forty-five-degree angle in both the horizontal and vertical planes from right to left. This is referred to as cross spot lighting. Cross spot lighting will not distort the natural tints of the face, the costume, or the shape of the light beam itself. Spot lights, therefore, should be located high enough from the pool deck to make this angle possible. Often it is necessary to build platforms for the spot lights because pools are not designed for the lighting needs of a water show.

Light that filters over the water from a height must not blind the spectator or create a glare on the water. Therefore, we suggest the lights be placed on the same side as the spectators.

When only two spot lights are used to illuminate the solo, duet, trio, or small group, the lighting technician should direct the light crew to adjust each light to the same shape and size and to gradually follow the movement of the swimmers. The light beam should not jump abruptly. When large groups are performing, the size of the light beam must be increased. Each light has a designated area of the pool it must illuminate. The following technique is effective. Divide the pool as a clock. Light number one will cover the area from twelve o'clock to three o'clock; light number two will cover three o'clock to six o'clock; light number three will cover six o'clock to nine o'clock; and light number four

[10] Ibid.

will cover nine o'clock to twelve o'clock. Each light should always be directed to cover the faces, legs, or arms of the swimmers when in the designated areas.

All deck movements are most effective when illuminated by spotlights. The light must throw a large enough beam to encompass all the swimmers. Overhead floodlights (sun guns) and underwater lights are usually added as the swimmers enter the water. The actual ceiling lights are very seldom turned on because these are house lights that announce the end of the show or the beginning of the intermission. Some pools equipped with overhead spotlights lend themselves to the use of these lights for special continuity skits staged directly in the beam of the fixed light. Other special-effects lighting may be created by extinguishing the underwater lights at a moment when the absence of light is a significant part of the sequence of the routine—for example, the death of Carmen or Lady Macbeth. However, care must be taken to insure the desired effect, changing the degree of the light, because such action could be immediately distracting to the audience.

It has been common practice to black out the lights as the swimmers make their entrances and exits from the pool. This is an irresponsible practice because swimmers become confused in the dark until their eyes adjust from being in the spotlight to being in complete darkness. Inevitably, accidents will occur during this period. Some form of light should be on at all times. To control the need for light, immediately following the completion of one routine, light the narrator, scenery pertaining to the next sequence, or the continuity skit at the opposite end of the pool from which the cast is moving. Although the spectators are aware of swimmers entering and exiting, a light illuminating something else will attract attention.

For the safety of the swimmers and the production crew, the national electrical code should be strictly followed and enforced. Professional electricians should be employed who are aware of the electrical loads of the circuits and the necessary care to be taken in laying the extension cords. Because water is a prime conductor of electricity, extreme caution must be taken in splicing cables around the pool area. The possibility of shocks, shorts, or electrocution is always present.

Another challenging aspect of lighting presents itself in the use of color to create a mood or to bathe the swimmer in an aesthetically pleasing atmosphere. Color may be used to suggest warmth or coolness, tragedy or comedy, day or night, gaiety or sorrowfulness. Warmth is felt in colors of amber, straw, pink, salmon, orange, or magenta. Cool colors are blue, white, and violet, whereas neutral colors are lavender, grey, and chocolate. Color media companies will provide color selector guides for light specifications and free color swatchbooks.

Color gels are used in spots or floods to bring out the skin tones, costume colors, and scenery accents. It must first be clearly understood that whenever white light is added to color, the color is washed out to white. Therefore, white should be used only with white. Because warm colors bring out the best skin tones, we suggest they be used for the water show. Some colors may be used effectively in combination: for example, pink with lavender, straw with pink, straw with green, magenta with pink or lavender. Green light has limited use, since it is unbecoming to the face and the hair. Blue-green is also a difficult color combination for the same reason; it gives a grotesque illusion. Great care should be taken in the use of red and blue: this combination does not create a warm hue; it cuts out the skin tones and dulls the colors of the costume. During the swimming routine, to usher in a different mood with the change in the music or pool pattern, colors may be changed. Sometimes this is effective at the end of the routine just at the moment the swimmers strike an ending pose.

As previously mentioned, underwater lights help the spectator to see the underwater action that takes place. These lights also add the third dimension to the pool. Because the underwater lights are generally white, it is difficult to use color above these lights; therefore, we recommend that the underwater lights be colored. This is not an insurmountable task. Heavy gels may be placed between the glass and the bulb in the underwater fixture. We suggest that these lights be colored pink or lavender, as these colors bring out the skin tones. The floodlights and spotlights on deck should be coordinated in color with the underwater lights so that the same colors are used on those portions of the body that are airborne.

Ultraviolet lighting creates a special effect that is appealing to the audience. These lights blackout everything except fluorescent materials, prints, and special makeup. Because these materials and the violet lights are expensive, care and preplanning are necessary to insure spectacular results worth the cost. At least two types of equipment are available. A 15-watt ultraviolet light has the capacity to project over an area of fifteen to twenty feet in a completely darkened pool, whereas an ultraviolet fluorescent tube will project only approximately eight feet. The 15-watt ultraviolet light takes five minutes to warm up, whereas the fluorescent bulb lights immediately. Either light will activate the fluorescent materials only when the materials are above the water. Anything under the water will be blackened out. Large fluorescent decorations placed on kick boards, flotation, and the heads or hands of swimmers will glow in the dark, giving the audience a special treat. Two or three 15-watt ultraviolet lights are enough to cover the completely darkened indoor pool.

Strob lighting provides an interesting allover effect to both deck and water movements. The strob light is a quickly timed on-and-off light that gives the illusion of a stop-and-go action. Strob lighting should not be overused, as it is tiring to the eyes of the spectators. One routine in a show using strob lighting is unique; more than one is distracting.

Body lights attached to the costume, flashlights or candles connected to dry-cell batteries are unique ways to use artificial lights. These may be connected so as to blink on and off or remain on during the total routine. When all other lights are off, these lights are readily detected by the audience and become an appreciated novelty.

Flashlights, battery candles, or burning torches held in the hand of the swimmer are special lighting devices. Torches create a safety hazard unless extinguished in metal pails that have been placed strategically around the deck. Flames must never be extinguished in the pool. Torches are wrapped in nonflammable materials and dipped in sterno. Sterno burns with little residue.

Well-trained and highly responsible lighting technicians are indispensable for adequate lighting. They should each be provided with cue sheets that note the starting point of each routine, the pool pattern, and the narration or music cue. Technicians can then write the exact lighting for each routine. It is a good idea to coordinate all light cues with all other portions of the show. Ample practice will provide appropriate and artistic lighting, creating a beautiful atmosphere and a professional production.

Makeup

Whether in artificial light or sunlight, performers use cosmetics to enhance facial expressions and present a healthy skin tone against which the eyes, eyebrows, cheeks, and lips can be accented. Because stage lights fade the nude complexion, it is necessary to dress up the face for either a natural look or for one that befits a character. Therefore, makeup for a water show must be closely coordinated with the lighting. Poor lighting can distort makeup that has been meticulously applied, whereas good lighting will bring out the qualities of the makeup that produce the desired effect.

Before applying makeup, analyze the facial characteristics to better understand the details of the face. Then, analyze the character or mood of the routine and select makeup accordingly. A study should be made of the available cosmetics that are dependable and waterproof. Be sure to follow the principles and purposes that guide the makeup artist. According to Vlastimil Boulilik in *The Art of Make-Up* the purpose of makeup is either to help the performer look natural in his role or to enhance the effect of his expression.[11] Some major principles to keep in mind when applying makeup are:

1. Because of the distance from stage to audience, makeup must be exaggerated to portray a natural look.
2. Makeup color should differ very slightly from skin color.
3. Makeup should maintain harmony with all other performers and costumes, i.e., soft colors, pale costumes, and soft makeup.
4. Illumination may distort colors; therefore, make proper adjustments by using the correct makeup; i.e., red tones in makeup do not show with red light.
5. Adjust the coloring of the actor's complexion to the lighting.

[11] Vlastimil Boulilik, *The Art of Make-Up* (Oxford, London: Pergamon Press, 1968).

THE APPLICATION OF MAKEUP

A room with plenty of light, multiple mirrors, chairs, and a table should be designated as the makeup room. A group may designate a makeup chairman, or each performer may be responsible for the application of her own makeup. To artistically apply cosmetics, enough time must be allowed to complete the task. Because the features of the face most readily noticed by the spectator are the eyes, nose, mouth, and lips, each must be carefully made up, beginning with a clean face after all old makeup has been removed. First, to the total face and onto the upper neck, apply a foundation and blend it well. Then, in sequence, make up the cheeks, eyes, eyebrows, and lips. Use powder to set the makeup. Once the makeup has been completed, caution the swimmers to keep their hands away from their faces. Because of the necessity to wear nose clips, just prior to the swimming routine, performers may wipe dry the small area on each side of the nose to which they then apply a liquid adhesive. The adhesive will become sticky for approximately one minute after it sets. The nose clips are then fit into place.

THE EYES

The eyes are the vehicles of the face through which emotion and feeling are expressed. Both eyes must be made up to look exactly alike. A tip to follow when doing your own eyes is (when right-handed) to make up the left eye first so the view is not blocked and there is less chance of smearing when making up the right eye.

Eye liner: Lines enlarge the eye and emphasize expression. They should be close to the lashes and extend to the outer corner, where they slant upwards toward the temple. The lower line should begin approximately at the middle of the lid and stop close to the outer corner. Line both lids with dark brown or dark grey pencil. Black is rarely used. The eyeliner should always correspond to the color of the eyebrows and lashes. The eye liner will appear softer after blue, blue-grey, or green eye shadow has been added to the eye makeup.

Eye shadow: Eye shadow should complement the color of the iris and change the expression of the eyes. It should be lighter than the iris. Dark eye shadow gives an unnatural appearance, whereas pastels complement the eyes. Pastel colors are grey-blue, grey-green, brown, slight gold or silverlustre. Select the color that is both compatible with the costume and the eyes. To prevent fading or darkening, it is recommended that a base of white, yellow, or pink (powder or cream) be applied to the eyelid before applying the eye shadow. Although cream or powder eye shadows are fairly dependable for use in the water, there may be a need to touch up the makeup before the finale.

The lashes: When the character of the routine calls for longer or thicker eyelashes, mascara should be applied. Use only waterproof mascara and apply sparingly to avoid stickiness. To make the lashes look longer and thicker, apply the mascara several times to the lashes, not waiting for each application to dry. As a finishing touch, carefully brush the lashes to make them smooth.

THE EYEBROW

Makeup is applied to the eyebrows after all other facial features have been completed. The eyebrow color should complement and correspond with the hair. Darken the eyebrows and shape them to complement the shape of the eyes, face, and lips. This completes the eye makeup.

THE LIPS

The lips and eyes are the two most important features of the face. Generally, makeup is applied to cover the natural lines of the lips. Only for special effects would this principle be altered. Lipstick should be applied thinly so that the lips when glossed have a natural moist appearance. The color of the lipstick must be compatible with the costume and complementary to the skin tone of the face.

THE CHEEKS

When cheek rouge is applied, the face, under illumination, takes on a fresh and natural appearance. Waterproof rouge or lipstick dotted on the cheek bones should be carefully blended throughout the cheek and upward toward the temple. This is especially true for oval-shaped faces. Persons with narrow faces should apply the rouge to the center of the cheekbone and blend throughout a small area toward the temple. When the audience is seated very near the water's edge, be certain to apply the rouge sparingly.

Upon completion of the makeup, look carefully into the mirror and evaluate the total effect, then solicit the appraisal of one or two other persons.

The back-stage makeup details run more smoothly when a chairman has been appointed. It is also extremely helpful to have one person in charge when it comes to obtaining the necessary cosmetic supplies (including cleansing creams and soft towels). Money can be saved for the club or for each performer by purchasing waterproof makeup and using it discretely and harmoniously to enhance the character and costume.

Properties and Scenery

To set the stage for the water show, properties ("props") and scenery are developed. The props are portable paraphernalia used in continuity skits, novelty acts, and individual routines, whereas the scenery is fixed in place either on deck or along the wall opposite the audience. Usually the scenery forms the basic background for all the routines. Its primary purpose it to enhance the general show theme and create an exciting atmosphere for the audience and the performances.

Props and scenery should be developed after a study of the following requirements for effective stage setting.

1. Scenery must give a clear image of the general show theme and enhance the desired effect.
2. All sets should be attractive, authentic in appearance, well designed and constructed.
3. The size and shape of the scenery should be in proportion to the wall space that is used and large enough to make a good showing from a distance. (Most audiences sit from twenty to thirty-five yards away from the scenery.)
4. Contrast, harmony, color, and proportions that are compatible with other props or scenery must guide the construction.
5. All props should be utilitarian, safe, and strong, and fulfill the purpose for which they were constructed.
6. All props and scenery should be waterproof, easily assembled and disassembled.
7. All props and scenery should be inherent to the overall production and be readily identified with it.[12]

It is a common practice to use one central backdrop as the focal point of the scenery. These backdrops are professionally painted and come in various sizes. A backdrop may be rented from a theatrical supply house in the area; the cost is approximately thirty-five dollars plus shipping. It is of prime importance to establish this budget in advance. Rented drops may normally be kept from eight to ten days. A special fixture with hangers must be attached to the pool ceiling from which the backdrop is hung. Once the fixture is installed, it may remain permanently in place and be used year after year. With few exceptions, backdrops depicting the central theme of your production can be obtained.

Often a scenery committee designs and constructs the scenery. This project is time-consuming and requires dedicated students who have a flair for designing, drawing, and lettering. However, since satisfaction and good companionship are gained through working on such a committee, the project is worthy of the time and effort spent. Care must be taken to see that the scenery is shared by enough students to keep the task relatively simple for all. A deadline for the completion of the scenery should be set at two weeks before the show. The scenery committee must also assume the responsibility for putting up the scenery and taking it down. The committee should find storage space for materials that are to be saved.

Because props are designed to fit the needs of a particular routine, they must be completed early enough to allow adequate practice time. Props are in

[12] Samuel Selden, *Stage Scenery and Lighting* (New York, F.S. Crofts and Co., 1930).

good taste when they are simple to use, yet effective during the routine. They must be sturdy enough to hold together for numerous rehearsals as well as look fresh during the actual production. When determining whether to use props, we suggest the student director consider the value of the props to her routine, the length of the time the props can be used once the routine begins, the cost, and the ease in clearing away for the routine that follows.

All props that are to be moved in place just prior to a routine must be moved quickly and quietly without disrupting the flow of the performance. A mark on the deck (masking tape) will enable the prop crew to locate the desired position.

When planning props, be sure there is adequate storage space at the pool so that the props will not be destroyed before the show by other groups who come in to use the pool.

All prop and scenery materials to be purchased or rented must be approved by the show director. The money for the necessary items usually comes from a general show fund.

The Dress Rehearsal

The dress rehearsal brings together the committee chairmen, spotlight crew, music coordinator, narrator, special acts, and the cast. Because of this large assemblage of people and props, each director in charge of a specific task must be organized for this event. One poorly organized director slows the progress of the rehearsal at the expense of everyone involved in the show.

To stave off a catastrophe at dress rehearsal, we recommend that the following details be planned.

1. The starting time for dress rehearsal should be announced eight to ten days in advance. Include the time the cast is expected to arrive. It is a good policy to send an information sheet with all necessary data to the homes of all those involved in the production.

2. All cosmetics must be purchased and a makeup section designated in the locker room. The makeup chairman should be someone the cast has met.

3. The lighting crew should be selected and commitments agreed upon. A planning session should be held to go over the show sequences and the orders for the light men to follow.

4. Cue cards and the script should be distributed to the narrator, music coordinator, and show director.

5. The printed program should be passed out to the total cast prior to the first dress rehearsal.

6. All costumes must be completed and tried in the water before dress rehearsal.

7. Student directors must inform their team, in advance, of their exits and entrances. All swimmers must know the proper entrance and exit for each routine.

8. The "bugs" must be worked out of the sound system so that a simple and rapid setup is possible for dress rehearsal.

9. All spotlights and special effects should be tried to see that the equipment works. Extra bulbs should be in stock.

10. Masking tape must be available for taping the extension cords.

11. The narrator should have practiced the script before the dress rehearsal using the same mike that is to be used during all other performances.

12. Scenery should have been hung and props put in place before the posted time to begin the dress rehearsal.

13. Other special equipment must be immediately accessible (flashlights, first aid, extension cords, scissors, wire clippers, and a ladder).

14. Special setups should be requested ahead of dress rehearsal (extra chairs for seating, bleachers opened, tables, etc.).

We suggest two rehearsals, each with a day of rest so that alterations, corrections, and improvements may be made without panic. When possible, we also recommend a day of rest between dress rehearsal and the actual performance; this psychologically gears the cast for the show. Swimmers of high school or college age quite often become exhausted from nervous tension and excitement; therefore, all effort should point toward a calm, well-organized atmosphere for the rehearsals and show.

The first dress rehearsal is expected to run more slowly, with time allowed for corrections, deletions, and minor additions. The second dress rehearsal is expected to flow more smoothly. Special groups may be encouraged to attend this rehearsal (those who cannot afford the admission fee or who cannot otherwise attend, such as senior citizens, mental health patients, handicapped people, or the mentally retarded). When possible, the cast should be permitted to view at least one or two dress rehearsals.

SUGGESTED PROCEDURES FOR THE FIRST DRESS REHEARSAL

1. Assemble and inform entire cast of organization and safety procedures.

2. Check communication system for direct operation to entire cast and working crew, i.e., light and sound technicians, narrator, and swimmers.

3. Check sound system operation and backup components.

4. Check light technicians' attendance and procedures.

5. Meet with swimmers, checking makeup, costumes, ticket sales, etc.

6. Assign one person to critique each routine as it is presented in rehearsal.

7. The first trial run-through must be slow and concise. We suggest the following procedure:

    a. Pool lights out; spotlight the narrator or some part of the scenery.

    b. Narrator speaks as swimmers move into place for routine A.

    c. Light the swimmers (no music); try gels until desired illumination effect is obtained.

    d. Lighting technicians record lighting cues on cue sheets for routine A.

    e. Lights out.

    f. Music, lights, and swimmers perform routine A again.

    g. Music and lights out.

    h. Repeat a, b, e, f, and g (this allows for immediate corrections for sound and light technicians and gives the swimmers an opportunity to accustom themselves to the lights.)

    i. Continue through the entire show in this manner.

    j. After completing this procedure, break and meet with the entire cast, making any necessary adjustments.

    k. When time permits, a second run-through is desirable as it tends to polish and smooth the ragged edges. This should be a straight run-through with no stops. One person is selected in each routine to wear a costume, plus all others who had any difficulty with a costume or headpiece.

    l. Upon the completion of the last routine, briefly meet with the cast and crew advising each of the need for rest, the starting time for the next scheduled session; and giving encouragement and support to all.

The second rehearsal is as near to the real show as possible. The cast is geared to project its personality because there is a viewing audience to entertain.

We suggest the second dress rehearsal be video taped if possible. The cast can be entertained later by watching the replay.

SUGGESTED PROCEDURES FOR THE SECOND DRESS REHEARSAL

1. Assemble all show personnel in locker room to inform them of announcements, operational and safety procedures.

2. Check makeup of swimmers, costumes, lights, etc.

3. Begin rehearsal—this rehearsal is conducted as if it were the actual performance, with no stops. Adjustments or corrections must be made immediately by direct communication, since any other communication would be disrupting to an audience (if present).

4. Complete rehearsal and assemble entire cast, giving additional instructions and praise where needed. Keep this short.

5. When video tape is used, this is the time for the replay. Assemble the group in front of the television, and they can be the audience. This is a great asset as there is immediate feedback from watching the production.

6. If there is no video tape and the director feels the cast would benefit from another rehearsal, carry it out, but with caution: the cast will be tired and will need rest. Many problems can be corrected without an entire rehearsal.

7. Praise swimmers and send them home with instructions regarding the the time of arrival for the opening night performance.

8. This could be a time to present each swimmer with a flower or some token. It can do a lot to raise tired spirits as well as add to the common bond they have achieved by working together. It also serves as an advertisement of the club, as the individuals display these tokens in school.

A dress rehearsal not only combines all the physical elements necessary to shape a production, but also adds the essential ingredient of people interacting with one another while satisfactorily fulfilling a common goal.

Physical Accommodations for Spectators and Swimmers

Final courtesies and accommodations add to the comfort and convenience of the audience and the cast.

When the pool is located indoors, the air temperature should be cooled for the comfort of the spectators. The cooling process will necessitate the termination of heat for whatever time span is necessary to cool the room. In addition to cooling the room, the water level must be raised and kept constant, to prevent unnecessary and distracting backwash noise and water splash sounds caused by the filtration and drainage systems. The water temperature must be at least eighty degrees.

Admittance to the natatorium should be accomplished with safety and ease. Ticket personnel and ushers, who are well versed in their responsibilities, should be on the scene at least one hour and a half before the designated starting time. Tickets should be collected at the door; however, the ticket sales booth should be a considerable distance down the hall from the balcony door. Programs are distributed at the door. When a full house is expected, ushers should urge the spectators to sit more closely together. Prior to the show, house lights must be on, to allow for safe bleacher seating. To create the mood for the show, soft background music may be played as the spectators are being seated. The cast and crew should be instructed to stay offstage once the spectators begin to arrive. Part of the surprise and pleasure is lost for the spectators if the costumes are shown before the act begins. The ushers will need to set aside some accessible seats to assist in the seating of late spectators. Another accommodation which should be provided is a coat-checking service. When coats are carried into the natatorium, they take up seating space; or if held on the lap, they may cause restlessness, especially among the children in the audience.

A performance should begin at the designated hour by a specified signal. The signal alerts all personnel to be in readiness for the starting time. Included are the light, prop, and music crews, the narrator and director, and the total cast, including the makeup and costume supervisors. When the spectators are seated and the cast is ready, the signal is given for the performance to begin. Following the applause at the conclusion of the finale, the cast should walk smartly offstage and proceed directly to the locker rooms. The manner in which the cast reacts to the ending of the show must be in good taste, happy but not boisterous, as good conduct adds to the professionalism of the production.

All costumes and equipment must be placed in readiness for the next performance. If this is the final performance, the set must be struck and all other items properly stored and inventoried.

AFTERWORD

When the house lights dim and the narrator begins the narration, all those who have contributed to the production will feel the excitement of being part of a tremendous undertaking. The component parts are about to be skillfully fitted together like pieces of a puzzle, and the finished product is ready to be enjoyed by the audience. Unseen, but ever present, are the attitudes and conduct formed by each individual who became a part of the total group effort.

FACTORS DETERMINING THE DIFFICULTY OF STABLE POSITIONS AND SCHOOLED FIGURE TRANSITIONS

Stable Positions

1. Amount of airborne weight supported during the balance of the position
2. Location of the center of gravity of the position
3. Degree of mechanical advantage to support the position

Schooled Figure Transitions

1. Amount of airborne weight supported during the transition
2. Degree of mechanical advantage to support and balance the body during the movement
    a. Distance traversed by each moving lever
    b. Length of each moving lever
    c. Weight of each moving lever
3. Resistance to movement in the water versus movement in the air
4. Location of the center of gravity immediately prior to the movement, during the movement, and immediately following the movement
5. Multiplicity of the movement, i.e., involvement of several levers, variety of muscle action needed for control
6. Duration of the movement

APPROXIMATE RELATIVE DIFFICULTY SCALE .1 TO .6

STABLE POSITIONS

Horizontal Group

Axial Group

APPROXIMATE RELATIVE DIFFICULTY SCALE .1 TO .6

SCHOOLED FIGURE TRANSITIONS
(Movement between stable positions)

Difficulty   .1

1. Back layout to back layout variant (flexion of one leg)
2. Back layout to back tuck open (flexion of both legs)
3. Back layout to back tuck closed (flexion of both legs and spine)
4. The reverse of these movements listed in 1, 2, 3 (extension)
5. Tub turn (propulsion of back tuck open around dorso-ventral axis)
6. Marlin (propulsion by scoops, pulls, and body roll)
7. Water Wheel (propulsion by bicycle action of legs)
8. Log roll (propulsion by a lateral body press)
9. Corkscrew (propulsion by a lateral body press)
10. Plank (propulsion by pulling the arms through the water)
11. Front layout to front layout variant (flexion of one leg)
12. Front layout to front tuck (flexion of legs and spine)
13. The reverse of these movements listed in 11, and 12 (extension)

Difficulty   .2

1. Propulsion of a back tuck closed to back tuck closed, as in a back somersault.

254

2. Propulsion of a front tuck through a front tuck, as in a front somersault.
3. Back tuck closed to back tuck tip up, as in a Kip
4. Oyster (flexion of legs at hips)
5. Submarine double ballet legs to submarine single ballet leg variant, as in a Heron

Difficulty .3

1. Segments of the Dolphin
   a. Back layout to axial one quarter of circle
   b. Traversing the circle from three to six o'clock
   c. Traversing the circle from six to nine o'clock
   d. Traversing the circle from nine to twelve o'clock
   e. Axial to back layout
2. Segments of the foot first Dolphin
   a. Back layout to axial one quarter of circle
   b. Traversing the circle from nine to six o'clock
   c. Traversing the circle from six to three o'clock
   d. Traversing the circle from three to twelve o'clock
   e. Axial to back layout
3. Segments of the Dolphin bent knee (as described in 1)
4. Segments of the foot first Dolphin bent knee (as described in 2)
5. Back layout to back pike axial, as in back pike somersault
   a. Propulsion of back pike axial until torso has rotated one half
   b. Propulsion of the last half of the back pike somersault
6. Front layout to front pike vertical, as in front pike somersault
   a. Propulsion of the front pike vertical through one half the somersault
   b. Propulsion of the front pike position until the torso is vertical and the legs horizontal (third quarter of somersault)
   c. Propulsion of front pike position until torso is horizontal in a front layout
   d. Propulsion of the legs from the three quarter mark to a front layout
7. The foot-first circle of the Dolpholina until a vertical low water line is established; from this position, propulsion of the low water line vertical to forward split vertical, as in a Dolpholina
8. Single ballet leg through a lateral body roll of ninety degrees, as in an Eiffel Tower; from this position, propulsion of the lateral layout ballet leg to front pike vertical as in an Eiffel Tower
9. The lateral body roll, used in the Dolphin figure eight
10. The lateral body roll used in the foot first Dolphin figure eight
11. Propulsion of a back layout to an axial alignment while descending head-first to a vertical low water line, as in a Contra-crane
12. Headfirst propulsion of a back layout to an axial position through a lateral body roll to a front pike vertical, as in an Albatross

13. Headfirst propulsion of a back layout to a split axial, as in a Walkover back

14. Static holding of a single ballet leg to single ballet leg submarine

15. Static holding of a submarine single ballet leg to single ballet leg

16. Propulsion of a front layout to a submarine double ballet legs position, as in forward pike somersault figures

17. Submarine double ballet legs to a submarine single ballet leg, as in Somersub

18. Propulsion of a submarine single ballet leg variant to vertical variant, as in a Heron

19. Propulsion of a back layout to a submarine double ballet legs, as in a Barracuda

20. Propulsion of a front pike vertical to a forward split vertical, as in an Eiffel Tower

21. Propulsion of a front pike vertical to a vertical variant, as in an Albatross

22. Twisting the low water line vertical

23. Twisting the low water line of a vertical variant, as in a Dolphin bent knee twist

24. Split axial to front layout, as in a Walkover back

25. Back layout variant to single ballet leg (extension of knee)

26. Single ballet leg to ballet leg variant (flexion of knee)

Difficulty   .4

1. Propulsion of a submarine single ballet leg through a lateral roll of 360 degrees, as in a single ballet leg roll

2. Submarine single ballet leg through a lateral and downward torso pivot to a forward split vertical, as in a Subalina

3. Forward split vertical to single ballet leg by means of a lateral and upward roll of the torso, as in a reverse Catalina

4. Forward split vertical to a high water line vertical, as in a Catalina

5. Forward split vertical to split axial (arc of legs), as in a Catalarc

6. Single ballet leg variant to vertical variant, as in a Flamingo bent knee

7. Twisting or spinning the vertical variant, as in a Heron

8. Twisting the forward split vertical

9. Spinning the vertical variant, as in an Albatross

10. Backward and upward propulsion of a forward split vertical to a single ballet leg, as in a Contra-crane

11. Foot-first propulsion of a single ballet leg to a submerged axial, as in a foot first Dolphin ballet leg

12. Submarine double ballet legs to vertical high water line, as in a Barracuda

13. Submarine double ballet legs to a split axial, as in the lateral pivot of the Gaviata
14. Vertical low water line to submarine double ballet legs, as in an Elevator
15. Front layout variant to an axial variant, as in a Swordfish

Difficulty .5
1. Submarine double ballet legs to submarine double ballet legs, as in a double ballet legs roll of 360 degrees
2. Submarine double ballet legs to reverse split axial, as in an Aurora
3. Back tuck open to double ballet legs, as in double ballet legs
4. Double ballet legs to back tuck open, as in double ballet legs
5. Front pike vertical to vertical high water line, as in a Porpoise
6. Double ballet legs to vertical high water line as in a Flamingo
7. Back tuck tip up to vertical high water line as in a Kip
8. Spinning the high water line vertical
9. Single ballet leg to axial variant, as in a Pirouette
10. Forward split vertical to reverse split axial, as in an Aurora open
11. Submarine double ballet legs through a pivot spin to a split axial, as in the Gaviata open 180 degrees
12. Single ballet leg to forward split vertical, as in a Crane
13. Front layout to forward split vertical, as in a Hightower
14. Opening and closing the legs in a high water line vertical, as in a split Kip
15. Front layout variant to a single ballet leg variant, as in the lateral pivot of the Swordalina
16. Front layout variant to single ballet leg, as in a Swordasub

Difficulty .6
1. Single ballet leg to forward split vertical, as in a Castle
2. Back layout to high water line vertical, as in a spiral
3. Forward split vertical to reverse split axial, as in an Aurora open 360 degrees
4. Single ballet leg to vertical variant, as in the Knight
5. Submarine single ballet leg through a lateral roll of 180 degrees followed by foot-first propulsion to a forward split vertical position, as in a Sub-crane
6. Foot-first propulsion of a single ballet leg around a foot first Dolphin circle

GLOSSARY

Abduction	Movement of the legs or arms away from the midline of the body.
Adduction	Movement of the legs or arms toward the midline of the body.
Arc	A curved aerial pattern of the legs made by moving one or both legs from pike to arch and vice versa, or the path taken by the torso and head (as one unit) as they press from horizontal to vertical.
Asymetrical patterns	Having unbalanced space and shape.
Axial position	That position in which the torso is either arched or curled forward.
Axial skeleton	Refers to the torso and head.
Axial, reverse split	A new name and new stable position in which the head, trunk, and one leg are vertical. The second leg lies upon the water surface, outstretched and to the back of the body.
Axial, split	A stable postion in which the torso and head are downward and perpendicular to the water surface, with the legs split front to back at the crotch to a nearly horizontal position.
Base derivation	Those positions that graduate in difficulty from the less difficult base or that graduate in complexity of design.

Base position	The position encountering minimal resistance, or that is simplest in design.
Bent knees	In this text, refers to a position in which both knees are flexed and held horizontal at the surface while the thighs, torso, and head are vertical.
Bottom depth	Refers to sculling in an area between the shoulders and beyond the head when the torso is vertical or arched.
Center of gravity	That point in the body about which all the parts of the body exactly balance each other.
Cervical arch	That area of the spine from the base of the skull to the shoulders (the neck) that is arched by hyperextension of the head.
Coda	A passage at the end of a composition of movement or music that brings it to a formal, complete close.
Contraction	A shortening of the muscle fibers.
Counter-balance	In this text, refers to opposing muscular forces that help to stabilize or hold a position.
Developmental movement	Movements prescribed to stretch and strengthen groups of muscles used in synchronized swimming.
Distal end	In this text, refers to one end of the muscles that move the knee, i.e., the end of the muscle that inserts about the knee causing it to extend.
Dorso-ventral axis	The axis of the body running from front to back.
Feathering	An application of pressure by the hands against the water, basically in one direction, while weaving them from left to right of that direction.
Figure	A sequence of movement that is described and listed in the synchronized swimming handbook of the AAU and that has been assigned a degree of difficulty.
Flexion	Bringing the distal parts of the body toward the face.
Horizontal position	That position of the body in which the torso is kept nearly parallel to the water surface.
Hybrid stroke	Parts of standard strokes combined to make a new stroke pattern.
Hyperextend	Stretching beyond full extension.
Interval training	Repeating a conditioning exercise with less time to rest between each effort.
Inverted **T**	A position of the arms when the torso is vertical (head downward) so that the upper arms are nearly parallel to the torso, with the elbows near the waist. The forearms are flexed at the elbows and the hands are positioned between the mid and lateral lines of the body and facing the pool floor.

Inverted, modified **L**	A position of the arms when the torso is vertical so that the upper arms are abducted until nearly horizontal, and the forearms are flexed at the elbows until vertical. The wrists may be at any degree of hyperextension.
Inverted **T**, *full range*	A position of the arms when the torso is vertical so that the arms are extended shoulder high to the lateral line of the body.
Inward rotation	Rotating the legs or arms inward.
Lateral line	An imaginary line running through the body, dividing it in two parts: the front and the back.
Layout position	That position in which the head, torso, and limbs are in line and horizontal along the water surface.
Lever of the body	A body segment capable of turning or moving around a fixed point, applying pressure to move a resisting force at another point.
Longitudinal axis	The axis of the body running from head to foot through the center, dividing the body into right and left halves.
Mechanical advantage	Refers to placing the support (hands) where the least effort is required to sustain the weight at the height desired.
Mid depth	In this text, refers to sculling in an area between the hips and shoulders when the torso is vertical or in a rounded axial (contracted spine).
Modified strokes	The standard swimming strokes as adapted to synchronized swimming.
Movement therapy	Exercises suggested to alleviate problems in movement or static holding of positions.
Muscle tension	Stress caused by the contraction of muscles.
Outward rotation	Rotating the legs or arms outward.
Pivot	Moving the torso and head from horizontal to vertical, or vice versa, by means of a hip rotation of one-half twist.
Plantar flexion	Moving the toes toward the sole of the foot.
Plumb line	In this text, refers to good body posture in which specific anatomical parts are in straight vertical alignment.
Popping up	Refers to swimmers surfacing at different times during a routine, causing an obvious mistake in timing.
Prone position	Lying on the water surface face downward.

Propulsion sculling	A constant pressure created by the hands in the water, in a prescribed pattern of movement, to change the depth of the body or to move it against resistance in an intended direction.
Protraction	In this book, refers to the rounding of the shoulders.
Recovery stage	Moving the arms through a line of least resistance, in the least amount of time, to a point of greater mechanical advantage.
Relative position	Refers to the placement of the hands for sculling in a position that best supports or propels the body.
Retraction	Refers to pressing the shoulders toward the back.
Scapula	The triangular bone of the shoulder girdle.
Schooled figure	Synonymous with figure.
Specific gravity	The ratio between the weight of any substance and that of an equal volume of water.
Speed-pattern sculling	Sculling rapidly to comply with the standard of eight patterns every five seconds.
Stable position	A position in the water that is in balance and supported, devoid of travel.
Supine position	Lying in the water on the back.
Support sculling	A constant pressure created by the hands in the water, in a prescribed pattern of movement, to keep the body at a constant level.
Surface transitions	In this text, refers to movements within the swim routine that enhance the flow of action and connect the choreographical phrases.
Symmetrical patterns	Surface patterns and designs in space that are balanced in shape.
Thoracic arch	Hyperextending that part of the spine from the neck to the waist line.
Top depth	In this text, when the body is horizontal, refers to sculling in the area very near the water surface with the arms along the sides of the body.
Variant position	A position in which only one leg is flexed at both the knee and hip joints.
Variation stroke	The addition of airborne patterns of movement to the recovery stage of standard strokes.
Vertical, forward split	A new name for a stable position in which the head, trunk, and one leg are vertical, and the second leg either parallel to the surface or slightly on an angle to the surface and extended to the front of the body.

Walking out   In this text, refers to those figures in which movement is toward the feet and to the back of the body. One leg, flexed at the hip and to the front of the body, is extended to the surface at the back of the body by means of an aerial arc, which may be horizontal or vertical.

BIBLIOGRAPHY

BENTHAM, FREDERICK, *The Art of Stage Lighting.* New York: Toplinger Publishing Co., 1968.

BROWN, MARGARET C., AND BETTY K. SOMMER, *Movement Education: Its Evolution and a Modern Approach.* Reading, Mass.: Addison-Wesley Publishing Company, 1969.

GUNDLING, BEULAH, *Exploring Aquatic Art.* Cedar Rapids, Iowa: International Academy of Aquatic Art, 1963.

H'DOUBLER, MARGARET N., *Dance, A Creative Art Experience.* Madison, Wis.: The University of Wisconsin Press, 1968.

ROCO COLOR MEDIA, *A Guide to Color Media Application to Theater Lighting.* Rosco Laboratories, Inc., Port Chester, New York, 10573.

SPEARS, BETTY, *Fundamentals of Synchronized Swimming* (3rd ed.). Minneapolis, Minn.: Burgess Publishing Company, 1966.

TORNEY, JOHN S., JR., AND ROBERT D. CLAYTON, *Aquatic Instruction.* Minneapolis, Minn.: Burgess Publishing Company, 1970.

INDEX